Unique containers are toy wagons and wheelbarrow. They're easily moved to take advantage of available sunlight or to escape unscheduled waterings on the terrace.

Raise
Vegetables,
Fruits and Herbs without a Garden

by

George "Doc" and Katy Abraham

Illustrated by Jean Helmer

Countryside
Books

About the authors

George "Doc" and Katy Abraman, famous for their "Green Thumb" column in 135 U.S. and Canadian Newspapers, were named America's Number 1 garden writers in 1973 by the Men's Garden Club of America.

A man and wife team at work for 30 years. Doc and Katy operated a commercial greenhouse and landscape business from their home in the Finger Lakes region of New York for 29 years. They host "Green Thumb" radio and TV programs in Rochester, N.Y. The radio program is in its 28th consecutive year. They also teach horticulture at Community College of Finger Lakes, contributed to the 1977 yearbook of the United States Department of Agriculture, and are winners of an International Society of Aboriculture special award in recognition of their outstanding service in promoting the value of plants to human life. They have written eight books.

"Don't confuse us with ivory tower horticulturalists," Doc stresses. "We've had out hands in the soil from the beginning and wouldn't have it any other way."

Obviously Doc and Katy have a way with plants. But more importantly for the rest of us, they have a way with words about plants and a commitment to spread the joy of gardening to everyone.

—the editors

Why this book was written

There are about 50 million home gardens in America today. Owners of these gardens are fortunate to have the land to grow crops.

But what about the millions of people in towns, apartments and inner cities with no space for a garden? A Gallup Poll taken in June 1973 revealed that there are 30 million such people in the United States who would raise a garden if they had even a tiny plot to till.

We have good news for these people. You can grow just about every vegetable, herb and fruit **without a traditional garden plot.** This book tells you how to raise them in containers and other small places almost anywhere and enjoy the same benefits a big garden yields:

the superior taste of fresh produce;

the satisfaction of growing your own food;

a real opportunity to beat the soaring cost of food and also raise special delights few can afford or find at the "super" market;

a healthful, dirt-cheap hobby the whole family can work at together at home.

Container gardens actually have some advantages over the traditional plot. You can move your barrels, tubs or pots for best exposure to the sun and access to water. Your garden won't have room for a weed problem, and it will be relatively pest free — you don't see many rabbits on apartment balconies.

We have attempted to cover every aspect of mini-gardening in this manual: container selection, soil mix, the best-suited varieties of vegetables, herbs and fruits, freezing and canning the harvest. The Green Thumb how-to tips are drawn from our direct, personal experience with each plant.

Gardening is nature's painless way to maintain good health and raise food to pep up a jaded appetite without hurting your pocketbook. Try it and see for yourself.

—George and Katherine Abraham
Naples, New York

Back Cover Photo — Compliments of Soil Blender® multi-purpose garden tool, manufactured by Garden Maid, Inc., Lebanon, Missouri.

First Printing, March, 1974
Revised Second Printing, January, 1975
Third Printing, September, 1977

CONTENTS

Farming the 17th Floor

High-rise apartment dwellers may think there's no room to raise food where they live, but that's not the case.

About a year ago, Organic Gardening and Farming (OGF) magazine ran a picture story on Manhattan farmer, Stewart Mott, who raises corn and 74 other crops atop the Park Avenue building where he resides. His farm includes vegetables, 26 kinds of berries, tree fruits and nuts, assorted herbs, cacti and flowers and shrubs.

"We've concluded there's nothing we can't grow," Mott told OGF editor M. C. Goldman.

Sweet corn, asparagus, carrots, cucumbers, blend right in with the soybeans, spinach, potatoes, rutabagas, peas and eggplant, trailed by vining squash, cantaloupes and watermelons.

Walnuts, apples, limes, cherries, figs and pecans shade the blueberries, grapes and avocados; while bananas, grapefruit, apricots and peaches back up the raspberries, strawberries, blackberries and boysenberries.

Mott raises 18 varieties of radishes, 22 varieties of tomatoes and 12 varieties of lettuce.

Even out-of-the-ordinary items work, like salsify, celeriac, coffee, mangels and even peanuts and wheat.

Mott told Goldman that he feeds his household and office staff along with two "farmhands" throughout the summer without buying any vegetables or greens.

He even has a high altitude compost bin against an outside wall, enclosed by cinder blocks. Plant trimmings, kitchen waste and manure from his two or three chickens (15 eggs a week) go into the heap.

Rooftop farmer Stewart Mott (above) tends part of his mid-Manhattan corn crop.

Container grown berry plants and fruit trees line the walk leading to one side of Mott's 17th floor farm in New York City (above right). Trailing vines, hanging plant baskets and strawberry barrels make full use of every inch of space.

"Farmhand" Chuck Phau (right) points out materials going into rooftop compost bin. Nothing is wasted. He asks tenants to save garbage for high-rise recycling.

Photos courtesy of
Organic Gardening and Farming Magazine

GROW CROPS IN CONTAINERS

Apartment dwellers, residents of a townhouse, or home owners who lack garden space should resort to the fastest growing trend in gardening — growing vegetables and fruits in containers. You'll be surprised to see what "concentrated" gardening can produce from vegetables, herbs, or fruits growing in containers. These can be anything from tubs, pots, baskets, boxes, tanks, barrels, galvanized pails or window boxes. Container-gardening is the answer to city apartment house dwellers who lack garden space, but hanker to "grow their own."

Farming on a window sill, balcony, rooftop, or a doorstep is the cheapest way to grow edible crops. You don't need a tractor, bags of fertilizer, tons of manure, a tool shed full of implements to get results. All you need for growing crops without a garden are some containers, soil, some seeds and a little plant food. We hope this book will help you get maxi results from your mini-garden.

There is another advantage to growing plants in containers and that is their ease of cultivation. These containers — whether they grow vegetables or fruits, are so small they can be turned or moved from time to time to take advantage of sunny spots so plants stay symmetrical in your window or sun porch, or patio. Large tubs can be used for containers, if mounted on a wheel platform so they can be moved from one spot to another. In fact, mobility is for some people the main reason for growing crops in pots or tubs or other containers. We have friends who grow a bushel of tomatoes and three pecks of cucumbers by moving half barrel containers mounted on wheels to take advantage of sunny places on their terrace as the sun changes position. In addition they harvested radishes, lettuce and carrots from boxes in childrens' wagons. Because of their shade trees, they had no spot in their yard where they would have enough sun to grow vegetables. To us, the main reason for growing crops in containers is the ease in caring for them. No weeding is required. Just feed and water uniformly.

Green Thumb Hints: If we had to put our finger on one of the big secrets for good growth of plants in any container — it's good drainage. No fruit or vegetable likes "wet feet" — gardeners' term for overwatering or poor drainage. If you use, wood, metal or earthen containers, be sure to drill holes in the bottom for good drainage. If water builds up from overwatering, or a heavy rain, plants will suffer from oxygen starvation. Use an electric drill to bore three or four holes (1/2 inch size is good) in the sides near the bottoms to let surplus water escape. We like to place pieces of crocks, pebbles or crushed stone in the bottom for better drainage.

Regardless of what you've selected for a container, a good soil mixture will be required. Our standard mix of 1 part each of sand, peat (or rotted compost) and loam works well. If your soil is heavy, add perlite, vermiculite, peatmoss or extra compost. Make your soil mixture a good one because it's going to last a whole season in a small area.

You will need to feed your plants more often in containers because the plants are in a confined area. We prefer to use a liquid plant food because it is more quickly available to the feeder roots. We apply one that can be used as a foliage feeding and then pour the solution over the entire plant allowing the run-off to soak into the soil.

However, any well balanced fertilizer will do. If you are an organic gardener use fish emulsion, plenty of compost and take advantage of rotted manure if it is available.

You have the choice of starting your own plants from seed, or buying started plants from a local nursery. Avoid heavy rooted crops such as corn (except dwarf), pumpkins and the like as they need more space for root growth. Peppers, cucumbers, melons, eggplant, tomatoes, lettuce, radishes, onions, beans, beets, and turnips are all suitable for farming in containers. Soil mixtures, fertilizers and starting plants from seed will be discussed in greater detail on the following pages.

CONTAINERS FOR MINI-GARDENING

Using various containers for growing fruits and vegetables is nothing new. The idea simply has been revived. Pictured in the tombs of the Pharoahs of Egypt are edible plants growing in tubs or pots. Ancient Chinese hosts would present their guests with dwarf kumquats ready for picking. Even the Lychee nut was grown in containers and shipped, in fruit, to wealthy Chinese. In France and England, it was the rage to grow fruit in containers to stretch the growing season. A gracious host would give his guests potted specimens bearing grapes, oranges or even bananas.

The type of container you use depends on what is available in your garage, kitchen, or basement. Here are some uncommon containers we've been using with excellent success.

GUTTER PIPE

Commonly called eaves trough. There are two kinds, the standard or half round and the more modern square or "K" type. We like the looks of the "K" type best. Either is simple to use. (1) Solder end caps on desired length of trough. (2) Drill a couple holes in bottom for drainage. (3) Fill with your favorite soil mixture (the 1 part each of sand, peat and loam is ideal). If your soil mixture is heavy, better add one inch of sand or gravel in the bottom of the trough before adding the soil. Place the trough on the edge of your patio, balcony or sidewalk, in full sun, if you plan on growing vegetables.

Water your plants according to the amount of rain you get. Heavy rains can fill the trough. If that happens gently tip the trough forward or backward and drain off excess. The secret during the growing season is to keep the soil uniformly moist. An occasional weed will pop up here and there, but they are rare. Container gardening is also work-free gardening.

Gutter Pipe

METAL OR WOOD BARRELS

Look around for a wooden or metal barrel that's been discarded. Just make sure the oil barrel is free from harmful chemical residues. If used for weedkillers or other chemicals, be sure to wash them and scrub the

Metal Barrel

insides with ammonia and soap suds. Ammonia deactivates most weedkillers. (1) If you use a metal barrel, have your garageman cut it in half, either lengthwise or widthwise, (2) have him burn a couple holes in the bottom for drainage. This is important since metal does not breathe or lose moisture from evaporation, as wood or clay containers do. (3) Sink or place barrel in among your evergreens. Or place it on your patio or balcony. Sometimes the barrel may leak from overwatering. If water stain poses a problem, put a plastic sheet underneath to catch any excess water. Use the same soil mixture recommended above — 1 part each of sand, peat and loam, dumped on top of an inch or so of gravel in the bottom. Plant seed or started plants. Because barrels are deeper than eaves troughs, you can grow squash, cucumbers, tomatoes, gourds, lettuce, radishes — just about anything you want. Vine crops need some support. We use four inch mesh concrete reinforcing material to let our cucumbers, and gourds ramble on.

Wooden barrels are still available in certain areas, especially around wineries. If you're lucky enough to latch on to a wooden barrel or a wine cask, you can get two containers for mini-gardening, simply by cutting the barrel in two, with a sabre or keyhole saw. If the bottom is rotten (or lacking) that's no problem, because it's not necessary. Don't trust your eye if you're going to saw the barrel in half. Make a chalk mark around it first, then you won't end up with one half of the barrel taller than the other. If the barrel has no bottom and if you use the barrel on the patio, place it on a platform.

Fill the barrel with our regular soil mix of 1 part each sand, peatmoss and loam. (see section on soil). If the barrel is where rain is apt to build up in it, better take the precaution of drilling a few holes in the sides and bottom for drainage. We grow the larger vegetables such as tomatoes, bush type squash, melons, cucumbers and eggplant. You can sow seed directly in the barrel, or buy started plants and set them in. Space them about one foot apart. Since the vines will want to climb, you can train them on a wire corset. Best material is four inch concrete reinforcing wire available from your lumber yard. Simply roll it into a cylinder and place it inside the round barrel. Sink it into the soil three or four inches and it will remain intact all summer.

If you grow stiff, woody plants such as blueberries or eggplant (these do fine in containers) you won't need a wire support.

WOODEN BOXES

Any kind of a wooden box will do for growing edible crops. If you can afford cypress or redwood, fine, but if not, use hemlock or any scrap boards you happen to fall heir to. Cypress and redwood costs more but last a long time. Since wood "breathes", wooden containers lose water faster than metal or porcelain types, so you'll have to water them more often.

Green Thumb Tips: Wooden boxes which are made of scrap lumber usually do not need drainage holes, however if the bottom is all of one piece you may need to drill two or three small holes in the bottom. If the box is ten or twelve inches deep a thin layer of small pebbles or

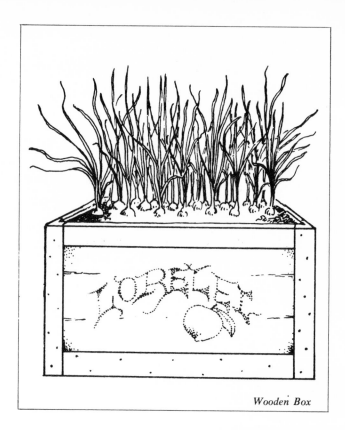

Wooden Box

coarse sand can be placed in the bottom before adding the soil mix. Use our standard soil mix mentioned above and place the box in full sun or on a platform which can be moved to sunny spots during the day. You can sow seed directly in the box or used started plants. Radishes, carrots, herbs, lettuce, onions, turnips, beets and other "smaller" growing vegetables do beautifully in boxes.

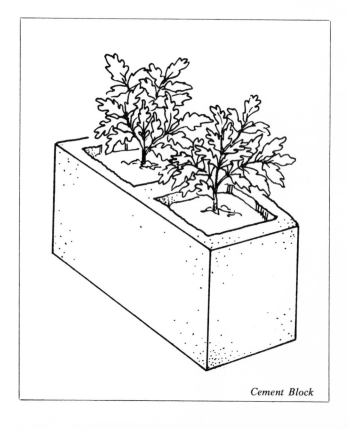

Cement Block

CEMENT BLOCKS

Nothing beats the cement block for growing herbs, onions, radishes and other "small" vegetable crops. Your lumber yard has all sizes, but an 8" x 8" x16" is easier to handle and holds moisture well. Place the blocks end to end so that the openings are vertical — facing the sky.

Green Thumb Tips: Fill the openings with standard 1-1-1 mixture, (sand, peat, loam) or if you wish you can add a bit more peatmoss since the blocks do lose moisture faster on hot days. Since the blocks themselves are quite porous no need to add drainage holes, or drainage materials in bottom. Plants to Grow: Ideal for green onions, (8 to a hole), carrots (6 to a hole), radishes (8 to a hole), beans (1 plant to a hole), chives, parsley, peppers, oregano and dozens of other herbs (one plant to a hole). On hot days the blocks should be watered well.

Troubles: Dry edges, around the leaves. Due to lack of water. Keep the soil uniformly moist. Curled leaves: Look for aphids, or spider mites. Syringe foliage. Don't use pesticides on any edible crops. Snip off any foliage that's dry, especially around the base of the plants.

GALVANIZED WATER TANKS

Galvanized Water Tank

Old galvanized water tanks are still kicking around in many barns or garages. If you happen to locate one, or plan to change your hot water system, get a welder to cut the tank, or "range boiler", as it's called by old timers, in two parts lengthwise. Let him burn a couple holes in the bottom. These tanks are five or six feet long and

make wonderful containers for growing plants in areas where tree roots are a problem. Just dig a shallow trench, set the tank in flush with the ground and the plants will grow lustily inside, laughing at greedy tree roots outside. We use these tanks for growing many kinds of herbs.

Green Thumb Tips: Be sure to place a small stone over the drainage holes to prevent earth from plugging up the drains. Fill with your regular soil mixture.

The Plants: Sow seed or insert started plants. Best items include herbs, dwarf tomatoes, lettuce, peppers, radishes, and green beans, carrots and onions. If you use pole beans be sure to use strings, fencing or wires for the vines to climb up on. Flowers are handsome and make an interesting addition to your landscape.

OLD CAR TIRES

Car Tire

We've finally found a use for old car tires. Grow plants in them! They work fine, especially if you have a slope and you want to raise blueberries. Drive an iron peg in the ground to anchor the tire, place plants inside and pour in sawdust or wood chips. Soak the plants well and you'll never have a weed problem, because the roots go down into the earth inside the tire. We've had wonderful luck growing blueberries and currants inside the tire.

MOP PAILS

Plastic mop pails, waste paper cans, garbage containers, (be sure to add drainage holes) and even clothes

Mop Pail

baskets with liners are good for your mini-gardening project. The purpose of plastic or aluminum foil liners is to keep the soil from sifting out. Generally speaking, care and culture is the same for most of them. While you can grow almost any kind of plant in a container, the secret is to choose the correct size. Some plants are easier to grow than others. We'll mention some of the easiest and best vegetables for you and your family, but don't hesitate to experiment and grow others.

Clay Pot

CLAY POTS

You can use a wide variety of plants in clay pots, glazed containers such as earthenware or whatever is available. We like clay pots because they breathe. They do dry out quicker than glazed containers or metal ones, and therefore should be watered more often. The reason? More than 50 per cent of the water applied to a clay container is lost due to evaporation. This means that plants in clay containers should be watered 50 per cent more than those in a non-porous container. Wooden containers hold moisture better than clay types but dry out more quickly than containers which are non-porous. All containers should have a few pebbles, broken pieces of pottery, or charcoal in the bottom for better drainage.

GARDENING ON A FENCE

If there's a wooden or iron fence on your property line, you're in luck! Use the fence to grow cucumbers, gourds or tomato plants. Most neighbors won't have any objections to your using the fence as a support for fresh vegetables. They can enjoy the fruits of your labors, while the plants take up only a few inches of actual ground space.

Green Thumb Hints: Set your plant next to the base of the fence after danger of frost is over. Or you can sow seed directly in the ground. Sow two or three seeds in spots which have been worked up thoroughly. Add peat moss if the soil is sandy or clayey. As the plants grow train them to climb vertically against the fence. You may have to use twistems or pieces of string to anchor the plants to the wire or wood. **Note:** Some people think that the wires on a fence get hot during the summer months and "burn" the vines of cucumbers or other crops. Not so.

Varieties of Tomatoes to grow: Cherry Tomato types. Try Pixie, Tiny Tim, Presto or Patio. Any of the small fruit tomatoes are ideal for fence gardening. Presto is a "large" cherry tomato about the diameter of a half dollar. Small Fry is another red "cherry" one inch in diameter. This hybrid bears enormous crops of round, bright red fruit and is resistant to both verticillium and fusarium disease. All small fruit tomatoes are worth growing on the fence, and will give your neighbors something to "groan" about. Red Cherry is a small bright red, the size of an ox-heart cherry. Red pear is pear shaped, one inch in diameter, and a mild flavor. Yellow pear is a tiny yellow fruit tomato, pear shaped and delicate. Yellow plum is ornamental as well as edible and looks fine hanging on a fence. If you want a large tomato try Moreton Hybrid or Burpee's Big Boy. (See Tomatoes for more information on mini-gardening.)

GROW CROPS IN TREES!

Who ever heard of growing pumpkins and squash in an evergreen tree? Several gardeners are doing just that. We saw a huge pumpkin vine trained up a White pine tree. The variety was Spookie, a small hard, bright orange-skinned pumpkin only six to seven inches in diameter. The sweet thick flesh is ideal for pies and the skin is attractive. Spookie yields great numbers of fruit and ripens earlier than the larger pumpkins. This small pumpkin is much better for "tree climbing" than the large types because it can be trained easier.

We've grown Lady Godiva up a Clump birch tree. If you're a pumpkin seed aficionado, try Lady Godiva, a new naked-seed variety. It grows to maturity in 110 days, the seed is hull-less, and delightful to eat, raw or roasted. Seed is highly nutritious, rich in proteins and requires no tedious shelling. The pumpkin weighs about six pounds and while the flesh is not the tastiest, it can be used for pies — just add a little bit more spice.

One gardener told us he grew "Golden Delicious" winter squash near his own evergreen. He sowed seed near his tree, and as the vines grew he trained them to grow up the trunk. The vine climbed up the tree and by fall it was loaded with beautiful bright red orange squash, a wonderful idea for folks who have no garden space. Incidentally, the Golden Delicious winter squash was developed specially for baby food, and this special strain has a richer orange, flesh color and higher Vitamin C content than other squash. The fruit is fairly large and pointed, bright orange outside and thick orange flesh inside. It's a fine-grained and well-flavored squash recommended for home use.

Bush Pumpkins: Did you ever hear of anyone growing pumpkins on "bushes?" Cinderella is a bush pumpkin producing big, ten inch Halloween pumpkins. You can grow it in among your evergreens or flowers in front of the house, since the plant only takes up six square feet. So, if you don't have a tree for your pumpkin vines to scamper up, grow the bush varieties. Sow seed on well drained land, and do not plant too early in spring.

Our Birch trees also support Concord Grape vines, giving us bumper crops of sweet grapes. Grapes are self-climbing and even if you can't find time to prune them, you'll still have enough fruit for your whole family — large clusters hanging up and down the tree.

Green Thumb Hints: Loosen up the soil around the base of your tree. About two or three feet from the base. Plant seeds in the soil, or set plants in ground direct. Keep the plants watered, and as soon as they start to "run" train the runners so they are heading up the trunk. To train a grape to climb your clump birch or other ornamental tree, it's simple. Set the grape root into the ground three feet from the base and keep it watered. When the first cane is long enough, train it to climb upward.

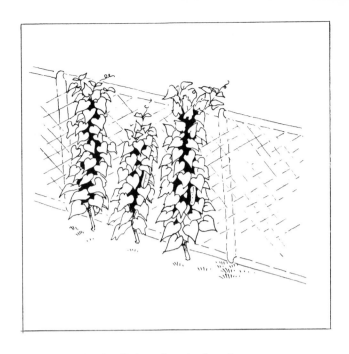

Vegetables that climb can be trained to a fence or up a tree trunk.

SOIL MIXES FOR CONTAINERS

People who "farm" in tubs, pots and other containers have an advantage over folks with conventional gardens. They can change and manipulate their soils a lot easier. Start out with a good soil mixture. You don't need a dozen complicated formulations.

Greenhouse operators use just one mix for a wide variety of plants, and there's no reason why you can't have one mixture for all of yours. The only exception is when you raise acid-loving plants such as blueberries. Such soils can be made acid by applying vinegar water, or by scattering some aluminum sulfate on the mixture. A good basic soil mixture for all your container plants is made up of 1 part peat moss, 1 part loam (which is ordinary garden soil) and 1 part sand. If you have access to compost substitute it for peatmoss. You'll see the above mixture referred to as a 1:1:1 mixture. Compost is excellent for building up soils and everyone who has the space should make his own (See Garbage Can Composting).

If you can get rotted horse or cow manure, substitute this for peatmoss. Other amendments include rotted leaves, and grass clippings. All add organic matter to the soil and thus provide both nutrients and a proper air-water relationship after feeding.

The type of soil you put in your container will determine the type of growth you'll get. A general rule of thumb is to use a mixture of equal parts sand, peat and loam. A heavier mixture may cause your plants to suffer from poor aeration. The reverse occurs in a soil that is too coarse — it will be sufficiently aerated, but may not retain enough water.

Materials such as sand, perlite, vermiculite, peat, sawdust, wood chips, bark or compost, are ideal for mixing with ordinary garden loam.

Because most containers range from 20 inches to less

1. The material needed for starting seedlings is either sterilized soil or vermiculite.

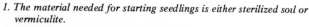

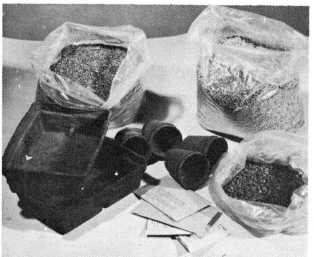

2. Press the moist planting medium firmly in the container.

3. Tap the seed packet with your forefinger to distribute the seed at the recommended rate on the label.

4. Cover large seeds with a layer of fine vermiculite. Leave small seeds uncovered.

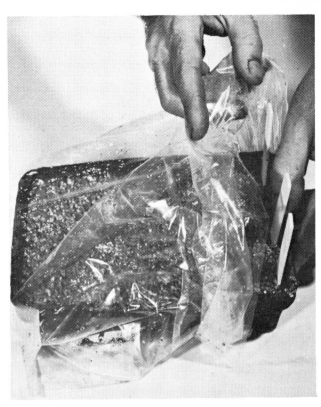

6. Place the seeded container in a polyethylene bag and keep it in a warm place until the seeds germinate. Then remove the bag and begin watering and fertilizing the seedlings.

5. Wet the seeded container until water runs out of the bottom.

7. When the plants are beginning to crowd, transplant the healthiest into permanent containers.

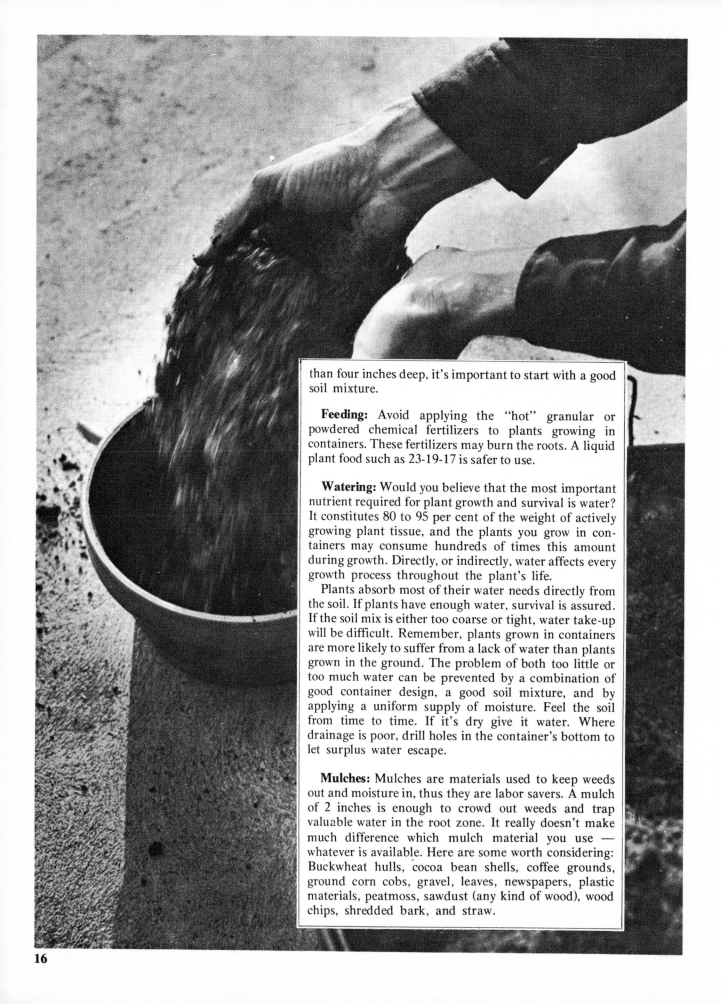

than four inches deep, it's important to start with a good soil mixture.

Feeding: Avoid applying the "hot" granular or powdered chemical fertilizers to plants growing in containers. These fertilizers may burn the roots. A liquid plant food such as 23-19-17 is safer to use.

Watering: Would you believe that the most important nutrient required for plant growth and survival is water? It constitutes 80 to 95 per cent of the weight of actively growing plant tissue, and the plants you grow in containers may consume hundreds of times this amount during growth. Directly, or indirectly, water affects every growth process throughout the plant's life.

Plants absorb most of their water needs directly from the soil. If plants have enough water, survival is assured. If the soil mix is either too coarse or tight, water take-up will be difficult. Remember, plants grown in containers are more likely to suffer from a lack of water than plants grown in the ground. The problem of both too little or too much water can be prevented by a combination of good container design, a good soil mixture, and by applying a uniform supply of moisture. Feel the soil from time to time. If it's dry give it water. Where drainage is poor, drill holes in the container's bottom to let surplus water escape.

Mulches: Mulches are materials used to keep weeds out and moisture in, thus they are labor savers. A mulch of 2 inches is enough to crowd out weeds and trap valuable water in the root zone. It really doesn't make much difference which mulch material you use — whatever is available. Here are some worth considering: Buckwheat hulls, cocoa bean shells, coffee grounds, ground corn cobs, gravel, leaves, newspapers, plastic materials, peatmoss, sawdust (any kind of wood), wood chips, shredded bark, and straw.

COMPOSTING

GARBAGE CAN COMPOSTING

Plants growing in pots, tubs or other containers need a soil mixture that's fairly high in organic matter. The organic material acts like a sponge and holds nutrients· and moisture so the potted plants can benefit from them longer. There are many sources of humus, such as rotted cow, horse or sheep manure. Or, you can buy peatmoss which is excellent as a soil conditioner. Probably, the cheapest and one of the best forms of humus is compost material. "Garbage Can Composting" is the answer for people in urban or suburban areas who wish to compost kitchen wastes, but have little room or cannot cover properly to discourage insects and animals. The Environmental Education Committee of Rochester, N.Y. passes along the following suggestions for making your own compost in a garbage can.

1. Take a galvanized garbage can with a lid which fits well and punch several small holes in the bottom.
2. Add three inches of good soil to the can.
3. Add some "angleworms" or some of the "red worms". (sometimes referred to as manure worms or red wrigglers). If drainage is good, the can may be sunk in the ground (to the level of the lid), allowing the earthworms to work all winter long below frost level. It can also be kept in a cellar, set up on two cement blocks with something beneath to catch any liquid draining out. This liquid is usually odorless and can be used on house plants, tubbed plants or garden plants.
4. Throw kitchen wastes into the can, to feed the worms.
5. Each addition of fresh garbage may be covered with a sprinkling of soil or shredded leaves, or grass clippings, but it is not necessary.

Odor is usually lacking, but coffee grounds are a natural deodorant and should be included. Worms thrive on them, too. If any odor should develop, a shredded newspaper will take care of it almost immediately. Grease will be tolerated in moderate amounts, as will meat scraps. Chicken bones can be added. They will add calcium and even if they don't break down immediately, they will return to the soil as filler.

One regular size garbage can will take care of a family of four, if the children are small. Some families start one can in the fall, then add another if this one fills up before spring, then they dump and start over. Others have two cans at the same time.

Note: Worms are not absolutely essential in making garbage compost, but they do help break down and enrich the finished product especially indoors. We recommend using them.

OUTDOOR COMPOST PILE

Where space is available outdoors, you can make compost bins from cement blocks, readily available from your lumber yard. Start the pile with leaves, grass clippings, weeds, or whatever is available. Then add table scraps, coffee grounds, tea leaves, orange skins, etc. Cover the pile with a two inch layer of manure — cow, chicken, horse, or material from the cat box. These manures are good sources of nitrogen. Continue to add the materials until the pile reaches a height of four or five feet. Turn the pile over (with a pitch fork or spade) after six weeks, and again in 12 weeks. Be sure the material is watered, as a wet pile breaks down faster than a dry one. Your pile will be ready for use in about four months. Some people do not turn their compost, but cover it with a black plastic sheet.

The basic factors which affect composting are moisture, air and size of particles added. The organisms which break down the compost use 20 to 30 times more carbon than nitrogen in the process of decomposition. While any type of organic matter will compost, a mixture of several types will give the best results. For example, leaves alone will break down, but if mixed with grass clippings, and/or manure, the decomposition rate will be accelerated and the texture and composition of the finished compost will be improved.

The secret to good composting is never letting the pile dry out. Moisture and oxygen are important if "soil bugs" are to decompose this material. A compost pile breaks down quicker in spring and summer. Some gardeners cover their pile with black plastic film during the winter to keep the heat in. The inside of a pile may become so hot a hand cannot be placed in it. It's not necessary to buy commercial activators to start decomposition. Fungi and bacteria are all ready there ... and will start breaking down the material. You might try to take a part of the old compost pile and place it on a new pile as a starter for the following year. If your village gathers leaves and hauls them to the dump each year, tell them you want some for your compost. It's a great way to build up a soil bank, for nothing is better for loosening up a heavy or clay soil, or adding to the moisture retention capacity of a sandy one.

Garbage can composter

STARTING YOUR PLANTS

If you have only a few containers in which to grow your plants, chances are you'll be better off to buy started plants from the greenhouse. However, many like to start their own, and since half the fun is in the growing, there is no reason why you can't start your own.

Starting Seeds: The best way to start seed is to begin with a good seed starting mix. Instant soils are on the

Make certain starting soil is high in organic matter. This will ensure the entry of oxygen and water into the medium.

When soil has been placed in the container, sow seed at the prescribed rate.

market, and these are loose, fluffy and ideal for seed starting.

Seeds of vine crops such as melons, cucumbers, squash and also eggplant should be sown, two or three seeds in a peat pot of this mixture or one seed per Jiffy-7 pellet. These crops resent transplanting so should be started in separate containers where they can be planted, pot and all, without disturbing roots. All other seeds can be started in boxes or large pots and transplanted after a couple of weeks to give each plant more room for growing.

The method is simple. Sow seed about one-fourth inch apart and cover lightly with peatmoss. A large clay pot or wooden box makes a fine container for starting. Water the container by placing it in a pan of water until soil is thoroughly soaked. Place a plastic sheet over the top or slip it inside a plastic bag. This traps heat inside and also saves moisture, eliminating the job of watering during germination. If you are unable to maintain at least a 72 degree temperature, day and night, invest in a small heating cable which can be laid zig-zag fashion in a box, with the seed flat or pot sitting on top of it. A plastic sheet is then stretched over the top of the box. Heat cables are inexpensive (from $2 to $5, depending on the size), and can make the difference between good or poor germination of seed. There are good seed starting kits on the market which have trays, pots, heat cable and plastic covers already to use. Trays can be left in daylight or darkness. After seed has started to sprout, move the tray to a bright window and remove plastic or glass covering.

When seedlings show their first true leaves (when about 1-1/2 or 2 inches high) they can be transplanted into boxes, two inches apart or separately into three inch clay pots.

Anyone who starts plants indoors should try using Jiffy-7 pellets. These are highly compressed pellets about 1/4 inch thick. You set them in a pan of water and they'll swell in minutes into a cyclinder about two inches high and 1-3/4 inches in diameter ... all ready to receive the seed. No pot is needed, since the growing medium is enclosed in a plastic net that holds its cylindrical shape. When ready, plant and pellet are set out in the garden or in the container with no shock or check in growth. The roots continue to grow through the net. The growing medium is sterile sphagnum peat with fertilizer added. Its excellent aeration and water-holding ability encourages vigorous plant growth.

When seeds are started in boxes or pots we put a layer of 1 part sand mixed with 1 part peat moss in the bottom. Then we fill the box with one of the prepared seed starting mixtures on the market. These include Jiffy Mix and Pro Mix which are light weight and sterile so that seedlings will not die from damping-off disease. We also use these mixes to fill peat pots when starting melons, cucumbers, eggplants, tomatoes etc.

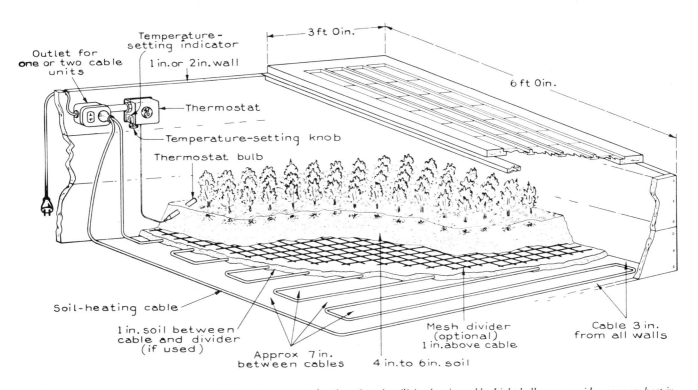

Outlet for **one** or two cable units

Temperature-setting indicator

1 in. or 2 in. wall

3 ft 0in.

6 ft 0in.

Thermostat

Temperature-setting knob

Thermostat bulb

Soil-heating cable

1 in. soil between cable and divider (if used)

Approx 7 in. between cables

4 in. to 6 in. soil

Mesh divider (optional) 1 in. above cable

Cable 3 in. from all walls

Cold frames are commonly used to start seed. Above is a cut-away drawing of a unit utilizing heating cable. Light bulbs can provide necessary heat in addition to illumination. These can either be placed along the side walls, as at left, or directly above the bed, right. The most economical construction is through the utilization of storm windows and doors.

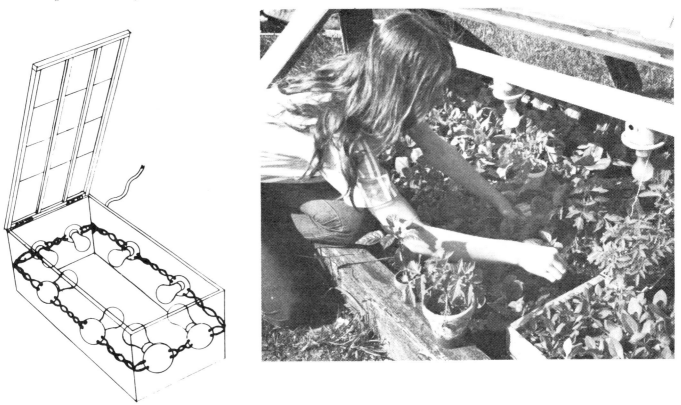

Methods of Support

Climbing or weak-stemmed fruits and vegetables require some artificial support.

A. Two posts support crossarms to which string or wire is looped over the top one, brought down and secured to the bottom.

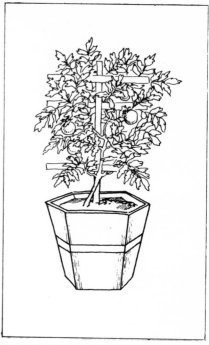

B. A single stake with crossarms supports a tomato plant.

D. Wire, decorative garden wire, or woven can be placed around the perimeter of a container, giving the plant necessary support.

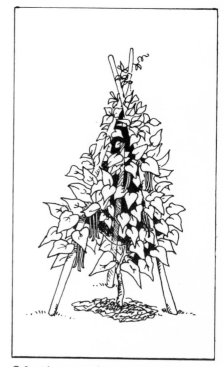

C. In wigwam fashion, three stakes are positioned so the plant is allowed to climb.

SPROUT GARDENS

Here's one type of gardening for which you don't even have to prepare a soil mix. Sprout gardens are the "in" thing today, and they are just the ticket for people who want fresh sprouts in their salads.

The Orientals have been masters of this art. Because this type of gardening was new to us we decided to give it a try. We took screw top Mason jars and used a small round screen for the lid (you can buy a screen or make one or use cheese cloth). The screen is for air. Next, we put about 1/4 cup of mung beans or other seeds in a jar of water, let them soak for a few hours, then drained the water off. A towel was wrapped around the jar to keep it dark, and the jar was placed on its side in a spot 70° to 72° F. The mung beans were rinsed in the morning and again in the evening, for each of four days. Shucks floated to the surface and were removed.

After sprouting, the beans were put in a colander where unsprouted seeds could be removed. Sprouts were cooked (stir fried), blanched, or eaten raw in salads. To keep them fresh, we stored them in a plastic dish in a refrigerator. One thing we found out is that many seeds will rot if left to stand in too much water. You can't crowd seeds too much, as it shuts off air, inducing spoilage. Sprouting should be done in a glass container for best results.

Here are some seeds home owners are using to grow healthy nutritious sprouts in their kitchens: Alfalfa, barley, buckwheat, red clover, cress, garbanzo, lentils, mung bean, mustard (black), oats (unhulled), radish (both red and black), soybeans, sunflower, and wheat.

Be sure to get seed from a supermarket or health food store. Don't use chemically treated seed.

INSECT AND DISEASE CONTROL

People who garden in containers or on rooftops can be thankful for one thing. They don't have to worry too much about fighting diseases and insects. That's another way of saying you don't need a cabinet full of high powered pesticides or an arsenal of spray guns.

Most insects can be controlled by spraying with soap and water, or handpicking. Safe insecticides for leaf chewing pests are nicotine sulfate, Sevin or Malathion. Malathion smells badly and you may not want to use it indoors.

Organic Gardener's Spray: Here's what's called an "all purpose" spray used by organic gardeners for controlling white fly, aphids, red spider mites and other pests. Chop 3 ounces of garlic bulbs (or use a garlic press) and soak them in 2 teaspoons of mineral oil for 24 hours. Slowly add 1 pint of water in which 1/4 ounce of oil-based soap has been dissolved and stir well. Strain and use.

Here's another one: Put through a grinder or blender three large onions, 1 whole garlic (not just the clove); 1 hot pepper pod or two tablespoons of cayenne pepper. Barely cover the mixture with water, and let it stand overnight. Put through sieve in the morning and mash it through. Then strain through a dish towel. Put the liquid in a 1 gallon jug and fill the jug to the top with water. Now it's ready to be used for spraying.

You can buy yourself an inexpensive hand sprayer, or use one of the plunger types which dispense window cleaners.

The following are insect and disease identification charts that will help you control pests that may attack your crops. Please consult your local garden center for a listing of commercial controls as regulations vary from state to state.

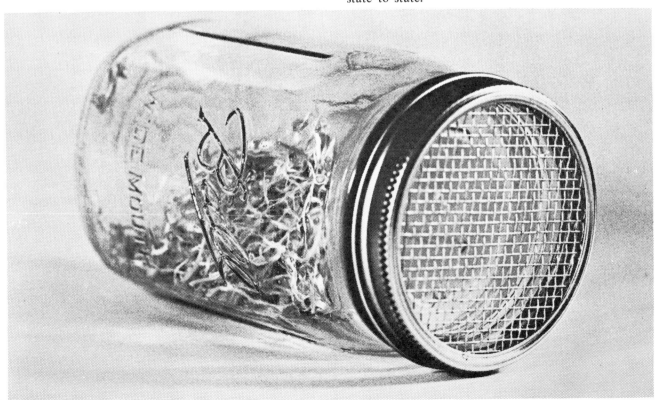

Vegetable Insect Identification Guide

Asparagus

Asparagus beetles
Leaves eaten and shoots channeled by greenish-gray larvae or dark beetle 1/4 inch long, with orange to yellow markings or reddish-tan beetles with 6 black spots on the back.

Bean

Bean leaf beetle
Circular holes eaten in leaves by yellowish or reddish beetles that have 6 black spots on the back.

Leafhopper and aphid
Tips of leaves become dry and brown. Active hopping and running insects suck sap from leaves. Black sucking insects on stem.

Mexican bean beetle
Lower surface of leaf eaten between veins, appearing skeletonized by copper-colored beetle with 16 black spots on back, or lemon-yellow larvae.

Thrips
Leaves and small pods scarred by small yellow to brown active insects.

Bean weevil
Holes in stored dry beans; small, dark snout beetles crawling over beans.

Cabbage, Cauliflower, Broccoli, Collards, Kohlrabi, Kale, Mustard, Turnip

Cabbage worms
Leaves with holes eaten by green larvae.

Cabbage maggot
See soil insects.

Cabbage aphid
Cupped, distorted leaves; small, greenish, soft-bodied insects in colonies on leaves.

Carrot, Parsnip

6-spotted leafhopper [vector of yellow virus]
Bitter carrots of poor texture with many lateral rootlets.

Carrot rust fly
Crown and root with rusty tunnels and white maggots

Carrot weevil
Fleshy root tunneled by larva with black head.

Cucumber, Cantaloupe, Pumpkin, Summer Squash, Watermelon

Striped or spotted cucumber beetle
Leaves, stems, flowers, fruit and roots fed upon by beetles and larvae (roots). Adults carry bacterial wilt.

Aphids
Small, soft-bodied insects in colonies on underside of leaves.

Onion

Onion thrips
Older leaves wither from scars caused by thrips feeding at base of leaves. Small, yellow, active insects present.

Pea

Aphid
Plant terminals deformed, leaflets cupped and twisted. Small, soft-bodied insect colonies present.

Potato

Colorado potato beetle
Defoliated plants with yellow and black striped oval beetles 3/8 inch long, larvae are brick red.

Leafhopper
Leaf margins turn brown and die. Active adults 1/8 inch long and greenish wedge-shaped nymphs on foliage.

Wireworms white grub
Plants stunted, roots cut by orange-tan wireworm larvae or large white grubs. Tubers often tunneled.

Flea beetle
See under Tomato.

Rhubarb

Rhubarb curculio [a snout beetle]
Stems oozing sap from small punctures made by a black snout beetle.

Squash, Pumpkin

Striped and spotted cucumber beetles
See under Cucumber.

Squash Bug
Plants wilted, yellow, eventually die. Brownish flat bug 5/8 inch long and gray nymphs with black legs suck sap from plants.

Squash vine borer
Sudden wilting of one or more runners. Holes in stem near base, with extruding refuse.

Sweet Corn

Corn flea beetle [vector of Stewart's wilt]
Quarter-inch scars along leaf margin.

Corn earworm
Corn kernels destroyed and silks cut off at tip of ear by green or brown robust larvae.

European corn borer
Stalks and ears tunneled by small, pale-colored larvae.

4-spotted fungus beetle
Black beetles, 1/4 inch long, with 4 yellow spots on back.

Tomato, Pepper, Eggplant

Flea beetles
Leaves with many small "shot holes."

Aphids and Whiteflies
Leaves shiny with honeydew. Plants lack vigor. Terminal growth may be distorted.

Variegated cutworm
Tomato fruits eaten by robust, dark-colored cutworm.

Tomato hornworm
Leaves eaten. Ground beneath plant littered with fecal pellets of large green worm with "horn."

Soil Insects

Ants, root aphids
Attack roots and cause damage by feeding on or tunneling in roots.

Carrot rust fly, carrot weevil
Small maggots or larvae tunnel throughout the fleshy root. Damage

usually most severe near crown.

Carrot grub
Parsnip and carrot show large holes gouged out of fleshy root.

Wireworm, corn rootworm, white grub
Attack roots and cause damage by feeding on or tunneling in the roots.

Cabbage maggot [also attacks radish], onion maggot
Plants sickly, stunted, the stem deformed. Severe in early spring when soil is cool and moist. Small legless white maggots attack main root and stem (or bulb) below surface of ground.

Cutworms
Young plants cut off near the soil surface.

Insects attacking several vegetable crops

Aphids
Soft-bodied, sucking insects ranging in color from green to black, reddish or brownish. Usually attack the more tender, green stems or undersides of leaves, causing leaves to curl.

4-spotted fungus beetle
Active black beetle with 4 yellow spots on back. Feeds on ripe and decaying fruits or vegetables.

Leafhoppers
Small, green, wedge-shaped, active hopping and running insects found on leaves. Insects suck sap, causing leaf tips to turn brown. Later the whole leaf may wither, turn brown and die.

Flea beetles
Small, black or sometimes striped beetles with hard shells. Jump like fleas. Small pin-size holes chewed in leaves.

Blister beetles
Long orange or dark yellow beetle with black stripes on wing covers, or gray with black wing covers. Completely defoliate plants.

Grasshoppers
Heavy feeders on many garden vegetables. Eat foliage and tender stems.

Red Spider
Minute reddish, yellowish or greenish 8-legged mites. Infested leaves become mottled, light colored or yellow. Webs and cast skins on leaves and stems are visible with aid of magnifying glass.

Garden slug [snail]
Slow-moving, soft-bodied, slimy shell-less snail. Thrives in wet weather and heavily mulched gardens. Eats leaves and fruits.

Vegetable Disease Identification Guide

Asparagus

Rust
Orange pustules turning reddish brown to black on stems and leaves.

Beans

Bacterial blight
Water-soaked spots and blotches on leaves, stem and pod irregular in shape. Brown with yellowish or red.

Mosaic
Variously mottled (shades of green and yellow) leaves and pods.

Anthracnose
Sunken, reddish brown to blackish spots on pods, dark reddish areas in leaf veins.

Seed rots
Plants emerge poorly, are weak and stunted.

Root and stem rots
Plants weak, stunted leaves yellow, plants may wilt and die, roots and stem at soil line discolored and decayed.

Cabbage, Cauliflower, Broccoli, Radish, Turnip, Kohlrabi

Fusarium yellows
Leaves turn yellow, curl and fall (bottom leaves first). Plants are stunted, brown streaks present in internal tissues of stem.

Black Leg
Light brown to tan spots on stems and leaves, contain small black dots (fruiting bodies of the causal fungus) leaves wilt, stem blackens and dies.

Black rot
Seedlings stunted, leaves yellow to brown, may fall early. Plants collapse; growth may be one-sided.

Club root
Leaves yellowish-wilt on hot days; plants stunted, may die; roots warty, clubbed.

Soft rot
Slimy, soft odorous rot of leaves and stem often follows other diseases and insect injury.

Carrot, Parsnip

Leaf blights
Outer leaves and petioles turn yellow, then brown. Variously colored dark spots; entire top may die.

Aster yellows
Inner leaves stunted and yellow; outer leaves bronzed to purple; root stunted, woody, hairy-rooted.

Root Knot Nematode
Roots Knotted, highly branched, plants may be unthrifty.

Cucumber, Melons, Pumpkins, Squash

Alternaria leaf spot
Small, angular, water-soaked spots turning yellow then brown. May enlarge and become zonate (target). Leaves wither, fall early (serious on muskmelon).

Anthracnose
Round to irregular-shaped reddish-brown to black spots on leaves, streaks on vines. Fruits may blacken and drop off. Leaves wither.

Bacterial Wilt
Vines rapidly wilt, wither and die. Slime-strands between cut surfaces of vine. (Watermelon is virtually immune).

Fusarium Wilt
Plants stunted, yellow. Leaves wilt and die. Discolored streaks in vascular tissue, roots decayed (most serious on watermelon).

Root Knot Nematode
Roots knotted, highly branched, plants may be unthrifty.

Lettuce, Endive

Soft Rots
Soft slimy odorous rots of leaves

Yellows
Center leaves dwarfed, distorted and yellowed. Plants dwarfed, bunch heads loose or do not form.

Onion

Bulb and neck rot
Leaves die early. Soft. Sunken areas in neck eventually spreading

into the bulb. Gray mold may appear on and between bulb scales.

Pink root

Seedlings wilt and die. Plants stunted, roots shriveled, pink to red leaves often die from tips.

Smudge

(Primarily on white varieties) Dark green to black smudged areas (often in a ring-pattern). Bulbs may shrivel or sprout prematurely in storage.

Smut

Elongated, blister-like streaks in seedling leaves or bulb scales, eventually filled with dark brown to black powdery masses of spores. Leaves may be distorted, plants stunted and may die if infected early.

Pea

Blights

During wet seasons, variously colored dark streaks on stems, round to irregularly shaped spots on leaves with dark centers and margins, sunken on pods.

Seed rots [damping-off]

Seedlings fail to emerge or are weak, wilt and collagse from rot at soil line or below.

Powdery Mildew

White to grayish powdery coating — usually on older plants. Leaves distorted, yellowed, may die. Plants may be dwarfed.

Viruses

Leaves mottled or spotted in various patterns. Plants dwarfed; may die. Leaves and/or pods distorted, flowers streaked.

Wilt

Yellow, dwarfed plants often wilt and die. Lower leaves affected first at about blossom time. Leaves small, distorted, curved downward. Plants may break over near the soil line. Roots decay.

Potato

Early Blight

Dark brown spots, often zonate (target) enlarging and may kill entire leaf on stems. Spots are rounded and sunken.

Late Blight

Rapidly eniarging water-soaked spots turning from dark green to purplish to dark brown or black areas on leaves, petioles and stems. Entire top may be killed in a few days. On tubers, purplish to dark brown, sunken, blotchy areas.

Scab

Superficial, rough, pitted and corky areas on tuber surface. Tubers may not store well.

Black Leg

Plants yellowish, stunted and wilting, upper leaves curled and stiff, stem bases dark at first, turning brown to black, slimy and rotted.

Ring Rot

Leaves mottled and rolled, stems erect, plants stunted, yellowish. Tubers may have a yellowish or brownish, cheesy ring about 1/4 inch beneath the surface.

Seed Piece Decay

Seed pieces decay in soil, especially when temperatures are low. Emerging plants stunted, yellow and weak, poor plant stand.

Viruses Mosaic Leafroll

Mottled pattern of various shades of green and yellow lower leaves rolled or cupped upward, stiff and leathery.

Purple top

Plants stunted, leaves rolled, stiff, shoots (tips) purplish or yellowish.

Rhubarb

Root and Crown Rot

Leaves turn yellow, wilt and die. Dark discolorations at lower ends of petioles. Moldy growth may be present in wet weather.

Leaf Spot

Round to irregularly shaped, variously colored spots. Affected tissue may fall out giving the leaf a ragged appearance.

Spinach

Blight [virus]

Plants dwarfed. Yellowed leaves may be thickened and brittle.

Fusarium yellows, wilt

Young plants stunted, wilt and die. Brown streaks in stem tissues, roots blacken and decay.

Sweet Potato

Black Rot

Pale, yellowish plants. Enlarging sunken black spots on underground stems and roots. Bitter tasting root, may be dry and corky.

Storage Rot

Variously colored and textured rotted areas. Potatoes shrink and eventually mumify, mold growth may be present.

Stem Rot

Brown to black areas at or near soil line, girdling the stem.

Soil rot or pox

Most severe under dry conditions. Plants dwarfed yellowish or pale. Potatoes deformed with roughened scabby, pitted, corky areas. Blackish, girdling spots on underground stems and roots.

Sweet Corn

Southern Corn Leaf Blight

On leaves, spots 1/4 to 1/2 inches wide by 1/2 to 3/4 inches long. Tan centers with reddish-brown margins and yellowish halos extending from the ends on husk, kernel and cobs, tan lesions 1- to 2-inches wide and 1-1/2 to 3 inches long extending into inner tissues. May assume a smoky-black appearance during wet weather.

Northern Corn Leaf Blight

Elongated grayish-green, turning tan or brown lesions usually on lower leaves. First affected tissues appear frosted.

Smut

Silvery to greenish-white galls on above-ground tissues. These may enlarge and contain masses of black powdery spores. When mature, plants may be barren.

Stewart's Wilt

Long white or yellowish streaks or spots in leaves, turning brown. Young plants stunted tassel prematurely.

Tomato, Pepper, Eggplant

Early Blight

Brown to black spots on leaves and stems may be zonate (target). Most damaging on lower leaves, first leaves turn yellow, collapse, plants appear defoliated. May form dark sunken leathery spots on stem end of fruit.

Late Blight

Rapidly enlarging water-soaked areas turning brown to black. Foliage soon withers and dies. Also affects fruits causing blotchy, greasy-appearing lesions which soon turn brown or black.

Root Knot Nematode

Roots knotted, highly branched, plants may be unthrifty.

Septoria Blight

Numerous small, rounded whitish spots with dark margins on all above-ground plant parts. Lower leaves first turn yellow, then drop.

Wilts

Plants stunted. Leaves wilt, turn yellow, wither and fall starting at base of plant. Dark discolorations present in vascular tissue. Roots may be rotted.

Bacterial spot

In wet seasons, small scabby spots with whitish areas on fruit which may be roughened, distorted and cracked. Greasy spots with yellow margins on leaves. Plants stunted; flowers blasted. Upper parts of plant may wilt.

A variety of containers will work. Note the many shapes in the above photo.

A starter container can be a grapefruit rind or egg shell.

Even a pail will grow crops. Peppers thrive in the metal pail, while the plastic bucket yields a bountiful crop of radishes.

VEGETABLES SUITABLE FOR CONTAINERS

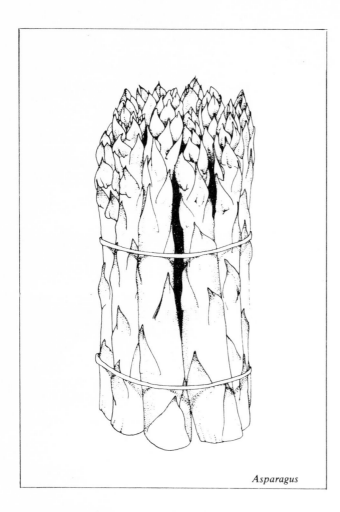

Asparagus

ASPARAGUS
(Asparagus officinalis)

You can find room for a few plants in the back of your floral garden, along the fence, or on the patio. Leaves make a fine lacy foliage plant which turns yellow in fall.

Green Thumb Tips: Soak seed in warm water for 24 hours, then plant. Allow about two seeds per inch. Cover with loose soil one half inch deep. Thin seedlings to two inches apart, and plant one in a 6-inch pot, or two in a 12-inch pot or plant in equal spaces right in the ground. Spread the roots before covering with soil. We like to start our patch with young root crowns. This saves a year over seed. Many nurseries sell the asparagus roots and these are all ready for planting. Do not bury the crowns too deeply — not more than two inches of soil over them.

Keep plants watered regularly and watch that tall, graceful fern-like foliage come up. This will be nice and green all summer, but will die down in fall.

Harvesting: The temptation will be great, but do not harvest any spears the first year. If you're like us, you'll break down and cut off a few spears the first year. It really won't do a great deal of harm. After the second year, you can cut crops for five or six weeks, and after the third year you can keep on cutting until July or August.

Troubles: Rust on plants and spears. Use the rust-resistant types such as Mary Washington, or "Waltham Washington".

Small spears, or lack of spears. Due to overcrowding. Divide the plants when spears get spindly, or feed the plants with balanced plant food in spring.

In fall, cut the tops back (once they start to yellow) and that's all the care they need. Some leave the tops on all winter, but the berries fall to the ground and new plants pop up all over the patch.

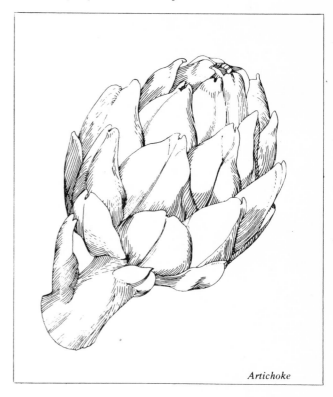

Artichoke

ARTICHOKE
(Cyanara cardunculus)

If you're hankering for a taste of the globe artichoke you can find room for this one in your foundation planting, or along the fence line. Don't devote precious container space to it, since the plant needs 3 feet up and about a 5 foot spread. Start seed in peat pots indoors, about 6 weeks before outdoor planting time.

Green Thumb Tips: Artichoke likes ample water, especially during a dry spell. The part of the globe artichoke used for food is the bud of the flower, which you pick before it is open. Of the large outer leaves only the small fleshy base is useful, but the center leaves are tender almost to the tip. The spiny center is called the "choke" and is not edible.

The Jerusalem artichoke (Helianthus tuberosus) is not an artichoke at all, and it has nothing to with Jerusalem. The name is a corruption of "girasole" — turning to the sun.

Actually, this is an American Sunflower, and the white tuberous roots are highly edible, safely eaten by diabetics. Roots sold in health food stores are inferior in flavor to the homegrown crop. You can put a few tubers of the Jerusalem artichoke along the fence and get heavy crops. Freezing improves flavor so dig as late as possible in fall or during a winter thaw.

Problems: Aphids may be bothersome. Spray with nicotine sulfate.

RECIPES

Jerusalem artichokes may be used in many different ways. You can use them in any way you use potatoes. They are excellent baked and one of the favorite ways of baking them is to put them in a shallow dripping pan filled with hot water. Put this pan on an asbestos mat to prevent their coming into direct contact with the bottom of the oven and bake slowly until they are soft. By immersing the tubers in warm water before baking, we have found they will bake more evenly.

FRIED ARTICHOKES: Peel large artichokes and cut the oblong pieces about 1/4 of an inch thick. Dip in flour and fry in deep fat.

SPECIAL ARTICHOKE SALAD: Chop equal parts of celery, green olives, green peppers and raw apples and cold boiled artichokes. Mix well and serve on a lettuce leaf with French Dressing. Sprinkle with grated cheese.

ARTICHOKE SALAD: One cup of raw artichokes chopped fine, one cup of raw carrots chopped fine, one cup of raw cabbage chopped fine and one cup of cottage cheese. Season to taste and mix well. Serve on slices of peeled onions or on a lettuce leaf with your favorite dressing.

ARTICHOKE PICKLES: Make them as you would your favorite cucumber pickles.

ARTICHOKE HAMBURGER STEAK. Use two pounds of chopped meat, 1 chopped onion, and four cooked artichokes. Mix well, form into cakes or desired shape and fry as you would hamburger. You may add a little water to the juice in the pan, thicken and serve as gravy.

ARTICHOKE BEEF STEW: Use your favorite beef stew recipe. Add artichokes about half an hour before serving.

BEANS

Beans are one vegetable that do well in any container. We know a family who let their children raise beans in window boxes in winter. How the kids go for the tender beans hanging from the plants.

Green Thumb Tips: Dwarf or bush varieties can be

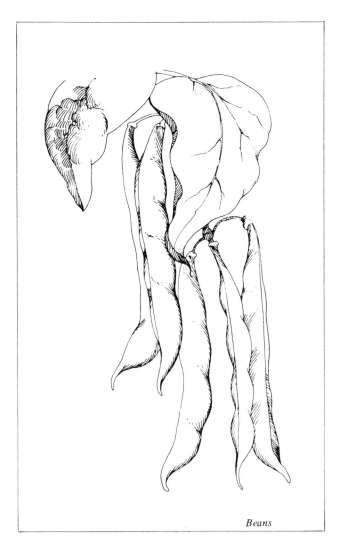

Beans

planted 3 or 4 seeds per sq. ft. of space. An 8 or 10-inch pot will support two bean plants. Drop the bean seed, eyes down, covering with 1 inch of soil. If planted 2 or 3 inches apart, no thinning will be needed. Beans are frost touchy so don't plant them outdoors too early. Seeds will rot in cold soil. If you're in a hurry about getting plants started, sow in peat pots and then set outdoors when soil is warm enough. Do not sow deeply — 1 inch is plenty, and cover with a loose soil. Crusting over means the seed cannot push through and you get no crops.

Snap beans come in both "pole" (meaning climbing types) or the "bush" or non-climbing. Pole beans can be planted in the ground or in containers next to your porch. The vines can be supported on strings or a trellis of some sort. If you have a porch railing, it makes an ideal support for beans. Or if you happen to have a stump in the backyard, cover it with a planting of beans. Plant bean seeds around the stump and train them to climb up strings fastened to the stump. We tried them next to our clump birch last year and it worked fine.

If you like lima beans, try the Thaxter, having bush vines. Fordhook U.S. 242 is another good bush lima, good fresh, canned, or frozen. If you want to train lima beans to climb up strings, try a pole lima such as King of the Garden. NOTE: Make sure you plant the bean seed eyes downward as it makes a difference in yield for all beans. Thin to 8 to 12 inches apart.

Problems: Brown spots on the pods. Might be anthracnose.

Control: Start out with disease-resistant varieties. Never weed, dust, cultivate or pick beans when they are wet, as this spreads disease.

Mexican Bean Beetle: Feeds on undersides of leaves. Control: Hand pick and burn. Look for the orange-colored egg masses underneath as this will reduce the beetle population before it gets started.

Bean Weevil: Mini-gardeners can raise good beans in a planter, or in a container only to have their surplus dry beans turn "buggy" or full of weevils during storage. Bean weevils can ruin jars of dry or shell beans, making them unfit for food or seed. The weevil begins its work by attacking the growing pods in the garden or container. When the dry beans are hulled and stored, they are already infested with the small white grubs. In storage the grubs mature and eat their way out of the dry beans, leaving small holes in the bean. Control: Store beans in cans and in an unheated spot (beans won't freeze). Or you can dip the beans in boiling water for 1 minute and then spread them out to dry. Or you can heat the beans in a shallow open container in an oven for 30 minutes at 130 degrees F. Bean seed can be heated to a temperature of from 130 to 145 degrees without affecting their germination.

Beet

28

BEETS
(Beta vulgaris)

Beets are easy to grow being tolerant of a wide range of conditions. Any type of container is suitable. Your foundation planting makes a good beet "garden". Beets are a "double header" vegetable, meaning you can eat the fleshy roots and tops. Young plants from thinning can make ideal beet greens, high in iron and vitamins.

Green Thumb Tips: Don't plant seed too thickly. Remember this point: Each compound beet seed is really a cluster with 2 to 4 seeds in it. Sow seeds so they are about 3 inches apart. Cover with 1/2 inch of soil. When plants are up, thin them to 12 or 14 plants per sq. foot of space. If you want to raise beets for greens only, sow the seed thickly. Feed and water to promote quick growth. They like to grow full speed ahead. The tops can be used when about 5 to 8 inches tall. If you want the beet "roots" harvest them when they are 1 to 1-1/2 inches across the tops, but roots can be harvested up to 3 inches. Small beets are better to eat than jumbo size, so you should make several sowings to keep new crops coming in. Surplus beets can be stored in a cool place, 40°-50°. If you want a novelty, grow the Burpee Golden (55 days), a yellow beet of good quality.

Problems: All tops, no bottoms. Due to close planting, lack of thinning or a lack of boron.

CANTALOUPE (see muskmelon)

CARROT
(Daucus carota)

Home grown carrots are a real treat. They are sweeter and more tender than store carrots. Low in calories, they are a great source of vitamin A, thiamine, riboflavin, and sugar.

Green Thumb Tips: Carrots are easy to grow in pots, tubs or in the flower border. Sow 3 or 4 seeds per inch, cover with 1/4" soil and after seedlings are up, thin the plants first to 3/4 inch apart. As carrots grow use the small ones (called fingerlings) by pulling every other one. Leave those you intend to grow larger in spaces 1-1/2" apart. You'll find that carrot seeds are slow to germinate. Place a plastic sheet or board over the row to trap heat in and hold moisture. Remove as soon as the seed starts to sprout. Don't forget to thin your carrots as soon as they come up, otherwise you will get all tops and no bottoms. Give carrots plenty of water on hot days. Prolonged hot weather and dry soils will retard growth and cause a strong flavor.

If you like only the tender young carrots or fingerlings, sow the seed thinly about 1/2 inch apart and do not thin out the plants. These little carrots will grow to about the size of your little finger and are great to eat raw or cooked. Make successive sowings every 3 weeks for a continuous supply of tender young carrots throughout the summer.

Nichols Garden Nursery has a system of raising carrots without using a spade or a hoe. It's a good idea for city dwellers and homeowners who have a "pocket patch" to garden in. Here's how it is done. Build a raised bed of 2" x 8" lumber (length optional) but width should not exceed 4 feet. Fill bed with 1/5 garden loam, 2/5 clean sand and 2/5 compost, rotted manure or peatmoss. For every 10-foot length of bed spread 5 lbs. of bonemeal. Mix thoroughly all ingredients, then rake down into a fine seed bed. Broadcast the carrot seed, cover with 1/4" fine sifted peatmoss. Water and keep bed well moistened, but not soggy. To harvest, pull carrots as they are ready. Sow seed in spring for summer crop. Sow seed in July for crops in fall. Carrots are easily grown in containers such as bushelbaskets, wooden boxes, or trays, clay pots, or cement blocks.

Problems: All tops and no bottoms due to failure to thin, seed sown too thickly. Strong flavor and poor growth due to too much heat or dry soil. Forked roots are due to heavy soils, or stony soil.

Carrot

CELERY
(Apium graveolens)

Celery is not a bread and butter crop for the gardener who lacks space. You can buy a dozen plants from your garden center and grow them in pots if you want to experiment. The number one requirement is lots of water.

Better devote your valuable space to other vegetables. Same advice for Celeriac or turnip-rooted Celery (Apium graveolens rapaceum).

Celery

CHARD, SWISS
(Beta vulgaris var. cicla)

Here's a very useful vegetable easily grown in pots, tubs or boxes, and small spaces in the flower bed. It takes hot and cold temperatures, rainy or dry weather. Many people like it better than spinach and call it a beet grown for its leaves.

Green Thumb Tips: Sow 1 or 2 seeds per inch, cover 1/2" deep and after seedlings are up, thin to 4 inches apart. Pull every other plant for use when 10 inches high, then let the others keep on growing. Cut out leaves for use so that new leaves will keep coming up from the center. If outer leaves are kept picked, the plants will produce until fall or early winter.

Note: With a little winter protection, swiss chard lives over and can be eaten as "spring greens" — at a time your body craves something fresh from the garden.

Problems: Very few, if grown in containers. If grown in the ground snails may bother but stale beer in shallow pans will catch the pests.

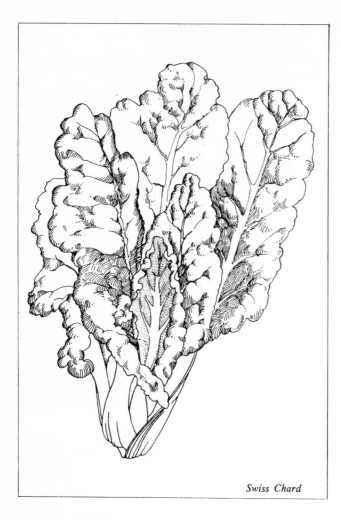

Swiss Chard

COLE CROPS

These include favorites such as **Cabbage** (Brassica oleracea), **Cauliflower** (Brassica oleracea var. botrytis), **Broccoli** (B. oleracea var. Italica) and **Brussels Sprouts** (B. oleracea var. gemmifera) plus **Kohlrabi, Chinese Cabbage, Kale,** and **Collards.** These items can be grown along the fence line, or in pots, tubs and boxes. For cabbage, kale and cauliflower, allow about 8 or 10 square inches per plant. Broccoli, brussels sprouts, kohlrabi and collards require 5 or 6 square inches per plant.

Some are highly ornamental such as ornamental kale and purple cabbage.

Green Thumb Tips: Buy started plants from a garden store or start seed indoors in peat pots. Set the transplants out after hard freeze danger is over. Cole crops are quite hardy and will take considerable frost. Do not let them grow dry, as it tends to make them woody. Plan on sowing seed about six weeks before you expect to set the plants in the open ground. When ordering seeds, look for the disease-resistant varieties to avoid yellows, a fungus which causes yellowing and dwarfing of cabbage and other cole crops.

Harvesting: Harvest cabbage when heads are large and mature. Harvest broccoli while the tiny edible heads are in tight bud stage. Plants will produce green flower buds way into the fall.

Care of brussels sprouts: When the tiny round "sprouts" form, break off lower leaves underneath them. The largest sprouts on bottom should be picked off and eaten and the plants will continue to produce more sprouts on up the stem until stopped by cold weather.

Harvest Cauliflower: It's important that the plants are not checked in growth at any time. They must be kept growing steadily and vigorously or the heads will be small and poor. When the heads start to form, and have reached a diameter of 2 to 3 inches, gather the large outside leaves together and pull them over the head, then tie together with rubber band or string. This protects them from weather and light and blanches the edible "curds". Harvest the head or "curds" when they are still compact, not open and ricey.

Harvesting Kohlrabi: Can be eaten raw or boiled. It is best tasting when grown in the cool days of spring or autumn and should be used when young and tender, not larger than a baseball.

Cabbage

Problems: All members of the cabbage family (cauliflower, broccoli, brussels sprouts, Kohlrabi and others) are susceptible to Club Root ("finger and toe" disease), a fungus which persists for many years in acid soil. As a mini-gardener who grows plants in containers, you're less apt to be troubled because you can easily change the soil, whereas gardeners who have a lot of land cannot. If you buy your plants from a greenhouse, make sure there are no lumps on roots. Many commercial growers are guilty of selling cabbage plants with clubfoot, because they raise the seedlings in the same soil year after year. Never set out plants having small swellings on roots.

Aphids: Spray with nicotine sulfate.

Cabbage looper: Eats holes in head. Handpick and burn, also spray with nicotine sulfate.

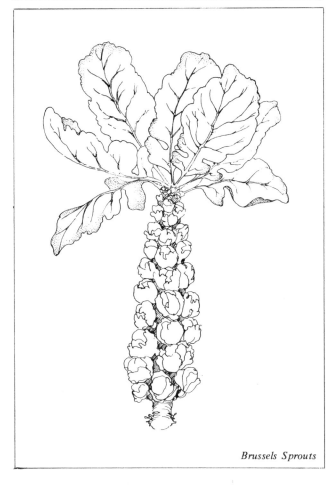

Broccoli

Brussels Sprouts

CORN, SWEET

(Zeá mays)

Where space is short, you can grow finger lickin' corn in less than 58 days from the time seed is sown. Grow the variety called Golden Midget, a hybrid with ears 4 inches long and 1 inch across with 8 rows of golden yellow, juicy kernels. Great for freezing on the cob because of its size and extra sweetness. Plants will grow 3 feet tall and usually produce two ears. There is also a white midget which is good eating but takes longer to grow.

Green Thumb Tips: Corn needs to be planted in blocks of 3 or 4, so a tub or box of plants is just right for cross pollination. Sow seed directly in the soil and thin seedlings so they are 4 inches apart. Make successive sowings so you will have ears all summer and fall. If more space is available grow Spring Gold or a Bi-color such as Sprite or Sweet Sue, or Seneca Chief.

Harvesting: Pick corn in the milk stage (will spurt milk when pressed with thumb nail) before it gets over-ripe and if possible not over half an hour before it is to be eaten.

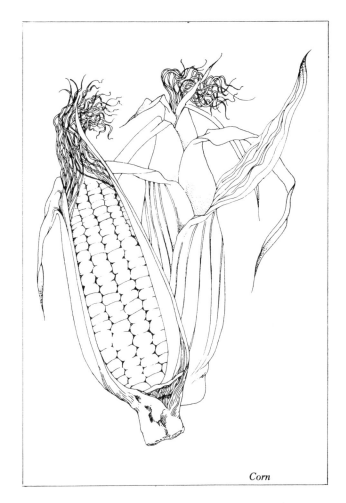

Corn

Problems: Corn borers and corn ear worms. Spray or dust the surplus plants with Sevin when corn is about 18 inches high. Direct the dust or spray down into the crown and the axils of leaves. Ear worm can be checked by spraying as soon as the silks begin to come out. Be careful to keep silks lightly but thoroughly covered.

CUCUMBERS

(Cucumis saturis)

If you really want to treat your family to something special — grow cucumbers on a porch trellis. If you have space they can be planted directly in a spot in the ground; if not, they do very well in tubs, half barrels, boxes or any container as long as you furnish strings, a trellis, or corset fence.

Green Thumb Tips: We sow seeds indoors in peat pots 1/2 inch deep 2 to 4 weeks before outdoor planting. However, you can sow them directly outdoors if you prefer. They will take that much longer to get a crop.

Cukes like a rich soil with rotted manure or compost added. For good growth allow about 8 to 10 square inches per plant. In the garden, or on the patio, cucumbers are pollinated by wind and insects. If you should want to try a dwarf variety in your house during the winter, you should transfer pollen with your finger tip from the male flower to the female flower. You can tell the female flowers because they have the tiny cukes forming after the blossom. If they are not pollinated they fall off.

If you have a touchy stomach and cannot eat ordinary cukes, better sow seed of the Burpless type. It's mild and not burpy. Lemon is a real cucumber which grows the size of a large lemon and has the same skin color. It's ideal for slicing and pickling.

Keep cucumbers watered regularly. And be sure to pick the cukes frequently, especially the pickle types, to keep the vines producing well. Outdoors it takes about 55 days to get a crop of cucumbers. The fewer cucumbers that are allowed to become oversized, the more vines will produce. When the crop is developing rapidly, pick 3 or 4 times a week. Don't disturb the vines when you harvest the crop.

Problems: Poor set. Can be due to lack of pollination. Cucumbers (and muskmelons) are "monoecious" plants, meaning the male and female flower parts are on separate flowers. The first 10 or 20 flowers that show up on the cucumber vine are male flowers, and there are generally 10 to 20 male flowers produced for each female flower. Male flowers are for pollination and naturally do not produce fruit. When you see blossoms drop, it's usually the males.

Bitter taste: It is natural to find a certain amount of bitterness in cucumbers. Dr. Henry Munger of Cornell University has produced a bitter-free cucumber, called Marketmore 70. Fluctuations in temperature affects cucumber flavor. You get the best flavor where there is no more than a 20 deg. variation. A sharp drop in temperature causes bitterness. Burpiness is associated with the variety, and perhaps the way the cucumber is grown. Beauticians like the bitter fluid in cucumbers and use it as a facial mask. Try giving yourself a facial by rubbing the cut end of a cucumber over your face. Note how it "tightens" the skin.

If you want to "de-burp" a cucumber, try this trick sent to us by a gardener. Take a good solid cucumber (any variety) and cut the top off, about 1/2 inch or so (stem end). Then gash the cuke and rub the cut stem end vigorously over the cut surface of the cucumber. When

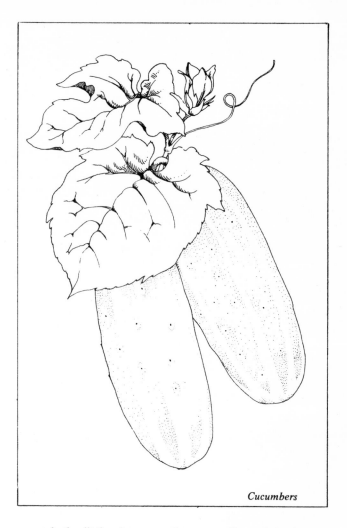

Cucumbers

you rub the little piece over the cut surface of the larger cucumber, you work the "bitter" fluid out of it. This bitterness fluid is what causes the burpiness and rubbing the two cut ends together draws it out.

A doctor who is also an organic gardener tells us that when you eat cucumbers, you should not peel them, as there is a deposit of magnesium underneath the skin. This magnesium counteracts the bitter factor and prevents the "talk back" or burpiness.

Problems: Misshapen fruits or nubbins: Curved fruit or fruit with constrictions at the stem end can be due to poor pollination or too high a temperature (over 90 degrees). Bacterial wilt or mosaic will also cause misshapen fruit. Best way to handle this is to grow varieties which are tolerant to some of the most serious cucumber diseases, such as scab, mosaic, and anthracnose. One such variety is Gemini, a hybrid of the modern gynoecious or all-female type. It starts to bear early, and like all cucumbers, if kept picked, continues to produce for weeks. Victory, an All-American winner also has wide tolerance to disease, including downy and powdery mildew.

Mottled Leaves: Due to mosaic disease. Leaves become a yellowish green color, plants stunted and wrinkled, fruits are runts instead of juicy cukes. Mosaic is carried by insects such as aphids and leafhoppers. Plant mosaic-resistant varieties such as Wisconsin SMR 12, Challenger, Saticoy Hybrid and Tablegreen.

DANDELION
(Taraxacum officinale)

The wild dandelion which grows in meadows and lawns tastes delicious but you can buy seeds of tame varieties which are even better. Various seed houses handle them and some of the varieties we have grown resemble endive. This great favorite for spring greens can be had over a long period and is grown as a pot herb in Europe.

Green Thumb Tips: Sow seeds in pots or tubs about 2 seeds per inch, thin and use young plants until you have 1 every 6 inches or so. Keep plants watered regularly and that is about all the care they need. The crop is harvested like spinach. You can blanch the leaves by tying them together, or cover with a tarpaper collar to exclude light. Blanching isn't necessary, but may improve flavor.

Problems: Bitter leaves. Some bitterness is natural. You can boil the leaves to improve flavor, but we prefer to tie leaves together so hearts are blanched and can be eaten like endive. A taste for bitter flavors is supposed to be a sign of highest sophistication. So develop a taste for Dandelions if you want to be sophisticated!

Dandelion

EGGPLANT
(Solanum Melongena)

Here's a vegetable that likes a lot of heat. They need a long season to mature the fruit. They grow extremely well in deep containers or among shrubs or flowers.

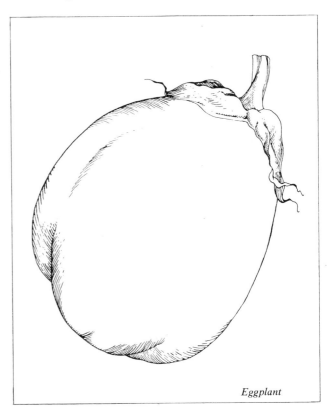

Eggplant

Green Thumb Tips: Eggplants like a soil rich with humus. The fruit is tastier if picked young, not over two-thirds of their full size. We like them when they are 6 or 7 inches long but some prefer them larger. Best variety is Black Magic hybrid, requiring 72 days to ripen from the time the plants are started from seed.

We start seeds in peat pots of peat moss mixed with sand or one of the prepared mixes. Sow 2 or 3 seeds per pot, cover 1/4 inch deep, about 3 weeks before planting outdoors. Then plant peat pot and all in container allowing about one square foot per peat pot of two or three plants. Note: Eggplant seeds will not come up unless the temperature is above 75 degrees, preferably 80 to 90 degrees for best germination. Eggplants do not transplant easily, so be careful not to break the roots.

You get a heavier crop if the fruits are removed before they reach full size, but they should be well colored and of good size before cutting. We wish more people would "discover" this wonderful vegetable.

ENDIVE
(Cichorium endivia)

Today, endive is eaten mainly as salad and takes the place of lettuce in many homes.

Green Thumb Tips: Similar to lettuce in culture. Sow seed about 1 inch apart and 1/4 inch deep and cover with peat moss. Thin and use small plants so that those remaining are 8 to 12 inches apart. You can buy finely curled or fringed-leaved varieties. A sowing can be made in fall and young plants can be moved to a coldframe as the crop will withstand light freezes. The broad-leaved varieties you see in supermarkets are grown as late fall and winter crops in the south, and shipped in a green or a partly blanched condition to northern markets as "escarole". The endive variety Florida Deep Heart is called Escarole and is considered the best broad-leaved endive. Green curled is a variety to use if you like the finely cut and curled leaves.

Blanching: Commercial growers and gardeners "blanch" endive to reduce the bitterness and to make them more tender. To some, blanching improves the appearance of the leaves when they are to be used for garnishing.

Here's a simple way to blanch endive: Gather the outer leaves together, using both hands, and wrap over the heart, then fasten them in place with a string or large rubber band. Takes about 2 weeks to blanch. Check them after two weeks or the crowns may start to decay.

Problems: Bitterness, cure by blanching the leaves. Snails eat holes in leaves. Scatter lime or wood ashes around each pot. Place dishes of beer nearby. Or spot check at night to catch snails in action. Rotted centers: Due to splashing water, or overcrowding.

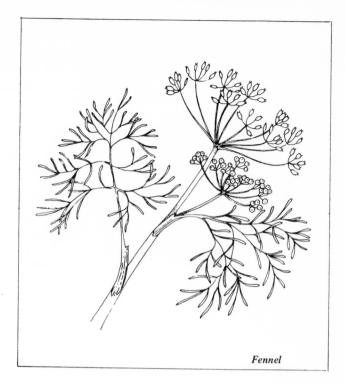

Fennel

GARLIC

(Allium sativum) (see onions)

Garlic

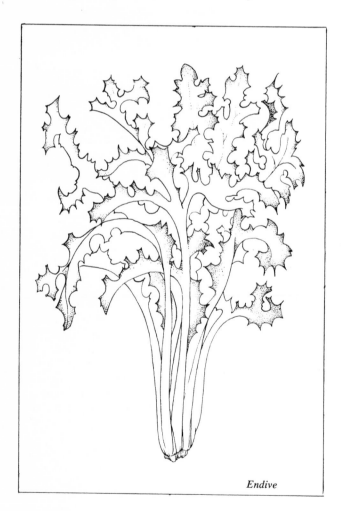

Endive

FENNEL

(Foeniculum officinalis) (see herbs)

KALE

(see cabbage)

KOHLRABI

(see cabbage)

34

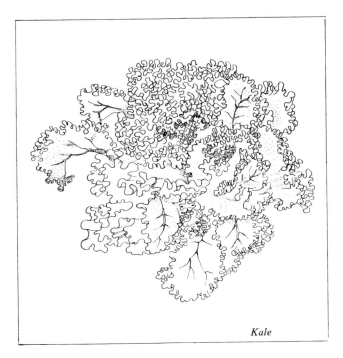

Kale

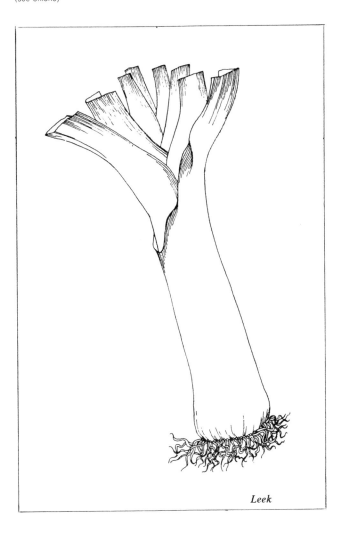

Leek

Kohlrabi

LETTUCE
(Lactuca sativa)

Without a doubt, lettuce is our most popular salad plant. It was mentioned by ancient writers as far back as 500 B.C. You have a choice of three types of lettuce: Head, cutting (also leaf), and cos. Our advice is to avoid the head lettuce in containers as it requires more space. Cos, Romaine types and Loose leaf types are better for small spaces. Some varieties "bolt" — that is go to seed early - and it is best to avoid them. Buttercrunch and Summer Bibb (cos types) are two good ones which won't go to seed readily, and they remain free from bitterness. Salad Bowl is an ideal looseleaf lettuce which holds its quality in spite of heat. Commercial growers use Slobolt, a crisp long-standing variety. We pick the outer leaves off when large enough, and the plants will keep on producing plenty of fresh green leaves. Bibb is another good one for containers, but we prefer the more improved Summer Bib.

Green Thumb Tips: Sow seeds 2 or 3 per inch in rows, 5 or 6 inches apart, cover with 1/8" peat moss. Thin seedlings (and use) until 5 or 6 inches apart for loose leaf, and about 7 or 8 inches for Bibb. If you want to try

35

head lettuce, grow them 12 inches apart, for heads need room. After the crop is harvested make another sowing of your favorite variety. You get good crisp lettuce when it is grown rapidly on humusy soil with plenty of moisture. Never let soil dry completely.

Problems: Snails: Put ring of sand or wood ashes around each plant. Check at night to catch them. Early or premature seeding. Due to heat or variety. Use slow-bolting types as Summer Bibb or Buttercrunch. Yellowing of foliage: due to too much lime. Lettuce likes neutral or slightly acid soil. Avoid deep cultivation, as root system is shallow. Grow in pots or tubs and avoid cultivation. Bottom Rot: Due to splashing water. Removing dead or dried leaves will prevent gray mold-rot and other fungus problems. Tip burn: Hot weather will cause tip burn, as well as dry soil. Bitterness: caused by variety, high temperature (especially at night).

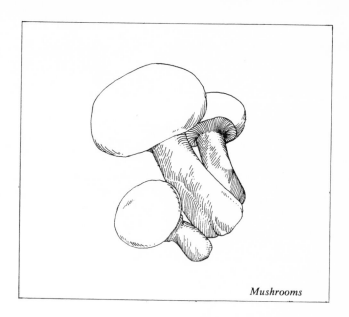

Mushrooms

Lettuce

MUSHROOMS

Here's a good chance to convert that dark space in your cellar or garage into something useful — mushroom culture. They like a temperature around 50 to 65 degrees, darkness and moisture (they are a fungus with no chlorophyl). We grow ours in trays of well composted manure, either horse or cow manure.

Under Glass Tips: Buy pure culture spawn from seed houses and sprinkle it over the rotted compost, place a piece of muslin cloth over the entire tray or bed, and water right over the cloth, repeating several times until

the soil surface is damp. After that, water twice a week and do not allow the beds to dry. Water the surface just enough to keep it moist but not soggy. Note: Try to maintain as cool a temperature as possible. If it gets over 75 degrees for any period, failure will result. If the air temperature drops below 50 degrees the crop will be delayed if not killed. Some gardeners use a barrel to grow mushrooms in. They fill the barrel with earth and horse manure and leave it in a corner of the house. A brick of mushroom spawn purchased from a garden center or seed house is broken into pieces the size of golf balls. These are worked into the manure-earth mixture, watered with tepid water by sprinkling can, and kept damp for several weeks. Gardeners tell us the mushrooms bear continuously for months, producing enough for their family and friends. They say that the second year, after the mushrooms rested, they came back again. Oddly enough when the soil mixture was dumped onto the compost pile or garden, the following year, rain and humid weather caused the little buttons to pop up again and they do it year after year. Note: if you plan to start your own mushroom bed, do not gather wild mushrooms for the spawn, unless you are sure of their identity.

MUSKMELON
(Cucumins melo)

The muskmelon, melon or cantaloupe makes a good item for your containers. Let's say they are all cantaloupes and belong to the Cucumis melo, except the cassaba and honey dew. All cantaloupes are musk-melons, but many types of muskmelons are not cantaloupes.

Green Thumb Tips: A wire trellis allows melons to grow vertically. Melons are heat lovers and do best in prolonged hot weather. Select varieties which are fusarium resistant, such as Delicious, Iroquois, or a hybrid known as Harper Hybrid. Harper is the best tasting of all melons we've grown indoors or outdoors.

Starting melon seeds is a trick. They need heat — 80 degrees or higher day and night. Your night temperature may go below this and the seed will rot before it can germinate. Here's a trick we use. Place an electric heating cable in a seed flat and cover with soil. Fill peat pots (or clay pots) with a mixture of 1 part each sand, peat, and loam. Place 2 or 3 melon seeds in each pot, cover with 1/4" soil and water thoroughly. A wooden frame with plastic sheet is placed over the seeds to trap heat inside. The extra heat germinates the melon seeds beautifully. You can get the same effect by starting them on a radiator. This works for other tough-to-start items such as peppers, and eggplants. Grow the melons on to a height of 3 inches, and carefully set them out in the container about 1 peat pot per square foot of space. Try not to disturb melon roots or any other member of the cucurbitacea family as they resent being disturbed or separated. It's difficult to transplant these items, as you would tomatoes, or other non-melon crops. The best soil for growing melons is one with plenty of well-rotted manure or compost. Keep the plants well watered, as they like it, especially on hot days. They do well trained up a trellis or porch pillar or stump. You can grow melons in tubs, if the vines can be trained on a wire trellis.

Harvesting: Pick melons when the body color turns to a yellow-green stage and the netting on the skin becomes rounded. Avoid the finger nail test which often induces rot to set in. The "half-slip" method of testing is reliable. Press lightly on the stem with your thumb at the point where the stem joins the fruit. If the disc slides off with just a little resistance, the melon is ready. Note: Cantaloupes will not develop additional sugar after they are picked, so do not pick them while green as they will never get sweet, although they will soften. The honey

dew melon has a sweet odor when ripe and a yellowish color to the skin.

Melon growing really is easy, but many beginners are discouraged because of the space they occupy. What few people seem to realize is that melons will grow happily up a trellis, and the heavy, ripening melons can be supported by "slings" of cloth to occupy no more space than a tomato plant.

Pride of Wisconsin is a fine, old-fashioned melon that fresh-fruit stands every year do a roaring business with. A dollar and more per melon is what many people will pay to sample its delicious sweet orange flesh, yet a packet of seeds costing a fraction less will plant dozens of vines — each vine capable of yielding eight or more luscious fruit.

Problems: Wilt, due to lack of water. Also to wilt organism spread by aphids. Screened greenhouses have no problems with wilt. Cassaba and honey dew melons have same care as other cantaloupes. Holes in skins due to snails or mice. Set mice traps, and inspect fruit at night for snails. Blossom drop: Nothing serious. The first blossoms on muskmelons are male, and are for rooster effect. A combination of male and female blossoms come later and it's the female flowers that produce. So don't be disappointed if not all your blossoms set fruit. The male blossoms will drop naturally. You can help nature by pollinating blooms indoors, since no insects or wind can help as it does outdoors.

MUSTARD GREENS
(Brassica)

Here's a dandy item for folks who want greens and have little space to grow them. Mustard greens are easily grown in crocks, pots or boxes and can be used raw in salads or cooked for greens.

Green Thumb Tips: Sow seed in a loose soil mixture and thin to 2 or 3 inches apart. Or set plants in pots, 3 inches apart. Make successive plantings. Burpee's Fordhook Fancy is recommended for its green leaves that curve backward like ostrich plumes.

You'll be interested in a Chinese Mustard (Bok Toi) with thick stems and green leaves that are chopped and added to meat dishes before serving. Or they can be lightly steamed with butter or a touch of bacon. The tender young leaves are fine in salads. Plant outdoors in early spring or late summer, matures in 60 days.

Problems: Spindly stems due to overcrowding. Thin plants to 2 or 3 inches apart.

OKRA
(Hibiscus esculentus)

If you're one who likes an okra dish (also called gumbo) but cannot make it because no okras are sold in your area, then devote some space to this member of the flowering hibiscus family. It likes heat so will flourish in

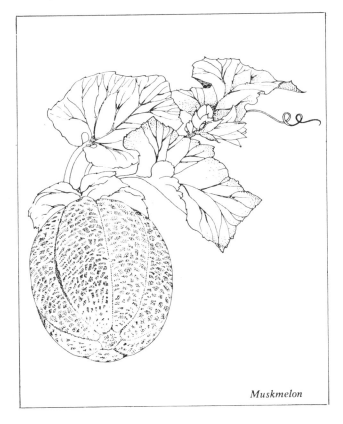

Muskmelon

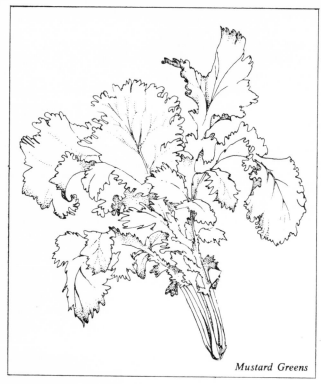

Mustard Greens

hot weather. Use the dwarf types as they take up less space than the large varieties. Grow in tubs or boxes. Okra is great for soups, and as a thickening agent and can be frozen.

Green Thumb Tips: Seeds are hard-coated so soak in warm water overnight to hasten germination. Sow seed 3 inches apart, cover 1/2 inch, then thin to about 1 foot apart. A 10" to 12" container will hold one plant. Keep plants watered regularly and when pod forms, pick while small and tender (2 or 3 inches ideal). Remove all mature pods so plants will bear continuously.

Problems: Bud drop, a common thing with all members of the Hibiscus family. Can also be due to hot, dry weather, change in temperature and poor drainage. Woody or tough okra, due to old pods, failure to pick regularly. Pick plants clean of any okra over 1-1/2 inch in size.

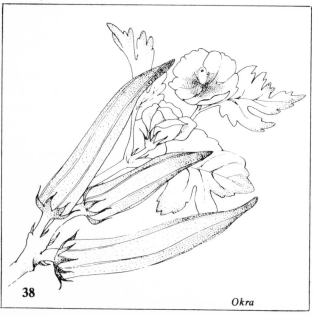

Okra

ONION
(Allium cepa)

Don't get the ornamental onion confused with the edible onion. Edible onions are grown from seed, sets (bulbets), or plants, depending on the purpose and the variety. It's hard to name another vegetable that does so much to pep up foods as onions.

Green Thumb Tips: To raise them from seed, sow thickly in pots or tubs, covering with about 1/4" of soil. Thin out to about 1" apart for small green onions and 3 or 4 inches for large mature bulbs. Use the thinnings for green onions or scallions and for salads and flavoring.

Onion Sets: Both early green bunching onions and large dry onions are readily raised from sets — small onion bulbs, 1/2" to 3/4" across. Sets are produced from seed the previous year. Plant sets early in spring about 2 inches apart in pots. If you want small early green onions, plant the set thicker, close enough so they touch one another. Cover sets completely with soil, and in a few weeks you can pull them for green onions. A good trick is to plant sets thickly then thin, using thinnings for green onions, leaving 2 or 3 inches between those remaining so that they will mature into large onions by July.

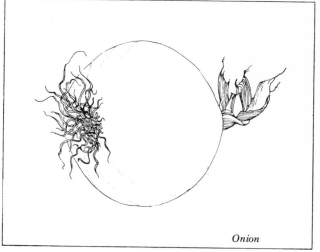

Onion

Smart gardeners make successive plantings of sets for green onions during the spring and early summer.

Onion Plants: You can even grow the big "hamburger" onions (Bermuda and Spanish onions) by setting out seedling onion plants early in spring. You can buy them in bunches in spring, ready to plant. Or you can raise your own by starting seed indoors in January in a bright window. When plants are 6 inches high, trim them back to 4 inches with shears. Set outdoors as early as possible, 2 or 3 inches apart. Spread roots out well when planting. Hamburger onion plants are cheap — a bunch running 55 to 110 plants per bunch. A couple bunches might cost you $1.50 or so ... well worth it.

Garlic: This member of the onion family is worth any space you can give it. It does best in any moderate soil. Buy a "bulb" from the supermarket and separate it into flakes or "cloves". Plant them 4" apart and about 2" deep. In late summer the tops begin to ripen and fall over. When this occurs, pull the bulbs and dry them like onions.

Here's a good trick for indoor gardeners: stick a wooden toothpick into a clove of garlic and place into a small glass of water. Soon it will start to grow. When you want a little fresh garlic, just snip the green part off. Keep adding water to the glass.

Leek: This unsung member of the onion family deserves more attention. Start plants early indoors, in spring. Set out as soon as possible. Make a trench 4" deep in evergreen border or along foundation of the house. Then set plants in, or set 5 plants in a 10" pot. Keep them well watered as they like moisture. Leeks will be ready to use in fall, and may be pulled and stored for winter. Or they may be eaten fresh in spring and summer, for soups, salads, egg dishes and casseroles.

Multiplier Onions: A small spot next to your home can be used to grow "multiplier" onions, hardy perennials planted in fall for early green onions. They are grown from top sets, sets that develop on top of the plant in July. May also be grown from divisions of clumps.

Shallots: Related to onions, this perennial is worth a spot or a potful next to the kitchen. This onion is started from sets planted in spring. Shallots mature in September, when they are harvested and stored in a cool, dry place. Small bulbs are compound and grow and break up into smaller ones.

Harvesting and storing: Most onions have tops which die down in fall. Pull them up and put into a garage to dry. Tops should be cut off, leaving 1 inch of stem on bulb. They can be stored in a dark place at around 40 degrees for a couple of weeks.

Problems: Onions and Shallots — Onion thrip, incorrectly called "thrip", and "onion louse", is a microscopic pest, causing "white blast", "white blight" and "silver top". Whitened leaves curl, crinkle and die. Control: Spray plants with nicotine sulfate.

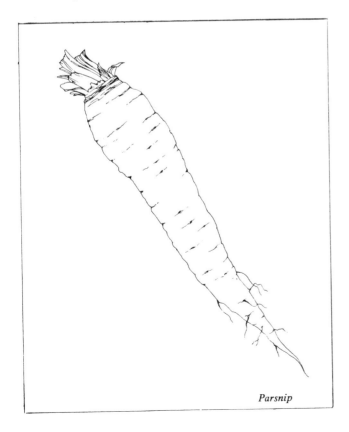

Parsnip

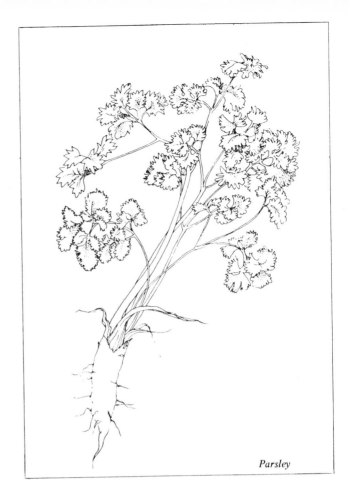

Parsley

PARSLEY

(see herbs)

PARSNIP

(Pastinaca sativa)

Here's one for the coldframe, during the fall and winter when it's normally idle. This fine vegetable is easy to grow and you shouldn't be without it.

Green Thumb Tips: We start seeds in our coldframe as soon as it is empty of bedding plants in the spring. Then we keep the plants watered right up until late fall. A raised bed surrounded by boards such as the one described under carrots raises fine parsnips.

Note: Parsnip seed is often tricky to start. Do not cover seed to deeply, as it has only a small amount of pushing up power. Cover lightly with peatmoss since deep covering is responsible for more failures than any other cause. You can mix a few radish seeds with it to break the crust. Make rows about 3 inches apart. Sow about 3 or 4 seeds per inch, then when plants are 2 inches tall, thin them to three inches apart and plant the ones pulled up in other spaces. Parsnip seedlings are small and not rugged, so handle with care. They like a loose soil of 1 part each of sand, peat and loam with another part compost mixed in.

Parsnips are extremely hardy. In the fall, they can be covered with leaves or straw, after the first freezing weather, and then they can be dug and used all during the winter months. Try some "french fried" parsnips and see if they aren't worth growing! Cold weather improves their flavor by changing the starch to sugar.

Problems: Failure of seed to germinate. Due to covering too deeply. All tops and no bottoms, due to not thinning out plants to 2 or 3 inches apart.

PEAS
(Pisum)

Most peas like cool temperatures. Use the variety called Wando, a small podded, high quality variety that produces fine peas even in a coldframe. Wando has dwarf sturdy vines, and pods are blunt, dark green and filled with tender peas. They grow in hot weather so you can make successive sowings right up until mid July. There are other good varieties but they should be planted early, even before frosts are over with to avoid hot weather.

Edible podded peas are a treat for the family. Peas can be eaten raw or cooked, pod and all, like green beans, or used in Chinese dishes. Pick pods when young, before the peas are lumpy. In fact, all peas keep their best quality for only a short time so pick them before pods get too fat. The higher the temperature the faster peas will pass the edible stage, so try to grow them as cool as possible.

Green Thumb Tips: Sow seeds in pots, or tubs, about 15 peas per square foot of space, cover with 1 to 2 inches deep. Keep them well watered after germination. Peas need support, such as trellis or chicken wire. If you raise them near your porch or a tree, string supports for the vines.

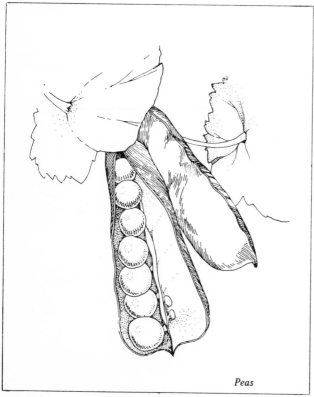

Peas

Problems: All vines, no pods. Temperature too hot. Hard pods, due to over age. Pick pods regularly. Make another sowing every 3 or 4 weeks so you'll have enough. Yellow, stunted, curled leaves. Due to aphids (plant lice). Spray with garlic juice or nicotine sulfate. Wilt: Due to fusarium fungus, causes rotting and distortion of leaflets. Grow resistant varieties such as Freezonian or Early Perfection.

Peanuts

PEANUTS
(Arachis hypogaea)

Peanuts in your mini-garden? Why not? They are a long season crop, like heat and can be an interesting item for children to watch and grow. The pods or nuts are formed underground. Soon after the flowers are pollinated, the short stalks which bear the blossoms become elongated and automatically bend down and push the small pods into the soil where it develops into a peanut. Don't grow too many as the vines take up quite a bit of space.

Green Thumb Tips: Buy nuts either in hulls or shelled, from a seed house. Shelled nuts can be placed 3 to 6 inches apart, but if in the hulls, plant about 8 inches apart. Cover with 1 inch of soil. You can use pots, tubs or boxes. Peanuts can be mostly for fun and pulling them up and seeing the big crop of nuts on the soil can be exciting. We roast our peanuts in a 300 to 350 degree oven for an hour, stirring frequently.

PEPPER

(Capsicum frutescens)

With peppers selling for 59 cents a pound in winter, it's all the more reason why you should grow your own. They can be grown indoors or out and are well adapted to containers. They take a long growing season and thrive on heat.

Green Thumb Tips: You can buy started plants from garden stores or start your own pepper plants from seed.

It's quite a trick getting pepper seed to germinate. They should be started indoors about 10 weeks before you intend to set plants outdoors. Sow seed in "Jiffy" pellets, peat, sand and loam, and cover lightly with peatmoss or sphagnum. Set seed flat in a pan of water and let it stand for half an hour. Sprinkle top lightly until wet, place pane of glass over it and keep it in the hottest part of the house. Pepper seeds like heat for germination. A heat cable in the bottom of a box, underneath the peat pots or seed box is excellent (see Starting Seeds). As soon as they start to sprout, remove the glass pane or plastic sleeve and bring to full light. If seedlings are in boxes, after they are about 2 inches high, transplant into large pots and set outdoors when danger of frost is over. Starting pepper seeds in "Jiffy 7" pellets or peat pots eliminates the chore of transplanting. Put two seeds in each pellet. If they both come up, remove one and transplant it to a pot, or give it to a friend. Plant pellets or peat pots in large containers outdoors after weather permits. One plant per 8 or 10 square inches is sufficient.

Note: Peppers do not have to be planted so they touch one another for peppers to set fruit. A single pepper will set fruit by itself, without benefit of a "rooster" pepper nearby. Failure to bear would be due to other causes, such as too high a temperature, or drying winds causing blossoms to drop, or too low a temperature so that blossoms don't set fruit. Certain varieties do better in some areas than others. Be sure to get the variety that has a growing season corresponding to that of your area. Don't let pepper color fool you. All red peppers are green before they are ripe and turn red or scarlet upon maturing. That red coloring is there all the while, masked by the nice green color. Of course, this does not apply to yellow types. Cut peppers off with a sharp knife, leaving a short piece of stem. This seems to protect the plant and also helps peppers last longer in storage.

As for variety, you have an advantage over the maxi-gardener, because he has to think of the growing season: "Will peppers, ripen before frost?" You can move your container indoors. Select California Wonder, Vinedale, Penn Wonder, Yolo Wonder — the list is endless. If you want one with yellow fruit, grow the Sweet Banana. Or, if you like hot peppers, try Hot Portugal, the best large hot red pepper. Rumanian Wax is a yellow fruited red pepper. (Hot!) And if you like the small red ones, try the Red Cherry, fruits are round 1 to 1-1/4" in diameter. It produces tremendous numbers of red hot fruit. Hungarian Wax is a hot pepper with bright waxy yellow fruit. The ornamental potted Christmas pepper, sold by florists as house plants, is red hot and edible! Save seed from it and plant just as you would the other peppers. Note: If you grow sweet peppers and hot ones side by

Pepper

side, don't save seed from the sweet ones for planting. The sweets and the hots cross over and the sweet pepper seed turns out to be hot, even though it looks sweet.

Problems: Very few when grown in containers. They may get white fly pest for which you can use the biological control, encarsia.

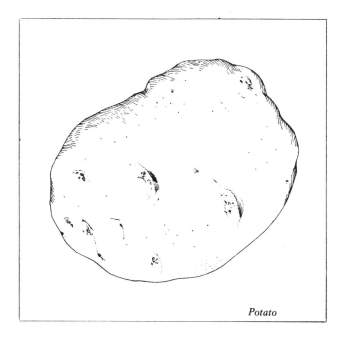

Potato

POTATO

(Solanum tuberosum)

Raise them in tubs, or boxes sitting on the edge of the

patio. A friend of ours raises potatoes in half barrels and trains them on a wire corset, just as you would tomato vines. Potatoes like a well-drained soil, one not too acid nor one too sweet. You can use "eating" potatoes to grow but it is better to contact a commercial grower for "seed tubers".

Potatoes Under Straw: You'll wrinkle your forehead when you learn you can raise a bumper crop of potatoes without digging up a lot of ground. The secret is to grow them under a mulch of straw, instead of in deep soil. It works. Growing potatoes in straw or hay is a method used most often when the soil is too rocky or thin. Here's how it is done: The soil is loosened with a hoe or rake. Use small potatoes or cut ones, the same as if you were planting in soil. Place the potatoes about 12 to 14 inches apart in both directions. Cover with about 6 or 8 inches of straw. If the weather is dry, water well, then wait for rain. Lime and bonemeal can be sprinkled on top of the straw if the soil is not rich or has not been limed. Note: One gardener tells us to place the "eyes" of the spud down against the soil, not up. Do not cover the seed pieces with soil — just straw or hay.

In a month's time you get tops about 12 inches above the straw. When you want to harvest potatoes, simply lift some straw and pick off as many tubers as you wish, then replace the straw. Harvest before frost. All you do is lift straw, pick the tubers and let the straw remain on the ground all winter. Next spring, chop up the straw into the soil, and plant your seed pieces on top of the soil and cover with straw.

You might like to try some red skinned varieties such as Red Pontiac, having shallow eyes and white flesh. Irish Cobbler is a popular early white spud and for a later variety try Russet Rural, Sebago, or Katahdin. Blue Victor is a large, round and blue-skinned, white flesh variety. Fingerlings is a yellow-fleshed potato, skin and flesh are both yellow.

Green Thumb Tips: Plant seed pieces 3 or 4 to a tub about 2 feet in diameter and 2 feet deep or 1 per square foot in a large pot, and cover 3 inches deep. These can be small potatoes from 1-1/4 to 2 ounces in weight, and planted whole. Larger potatoes can be cut into blocky pieces about 1-1/2 ounces each. Be sure there is one "eye" (bud) on each piece. If you want to try a few in a coldframe or among evergreens or flowers, plant seed pieces 18 inches apart and 3 inches deep. It takes about 30 to 40 pounds of "seed pieces" to raise 7 or 8 bushels of spuds. We don't recommend using up a lot of space on potatoes, but there is no reason why you shouldn't try some.

Problems: You can prevent a lot of them by using certified seed tubers only. Green skinned potatoes. Due to too much light. Cover roots with more soil or lay black plastic strips around the base of plants to keep out light.

POTATO, SWEET

(Ipomoea batatas)

This food crop should be trained on a trellis or wire fence. Try growing them in large pots or tubs along a

fence or around a tree. Good varieties include Orange-Jersey, Orange Little-Stem and Nemagold. New Centennial is a sweet, golden variety with copper skin, orange flesh. All-Gold Bunch Puerto Rico is one we think you should try in a pocket garden because it hasn't vines to run all over. You might try this one among your shrubs or evergreens. In tubs or boxes you may not get the root size you get from plants in a garden because this starchy tuber likes a deep soil. But they will be tasty and an attractive plant to grow.

Green Thumb Tips: Start sweet potatoes from plants. Plant two or three in a wooden box or tub, allowing about 8 square inches per plant. The container should be at least one foot deep. Or if grown in the ground, set each plant about 18 inches apart. Store sweet potatoes can be started in pots — some may sprout, and some may not. If they have been treated with a hormone to prevent sprouting in storage, you'll have a hard time breaking the dormancy. Better order plants from a seed house. A friend of ours uses his sunny bay window to start his sweet potato plants for outdoor growing. In January he gets a good sized sweet potato from the store, puts it in water, and allows it to grow into decorative vines. About June 1st he divides the vines taking each one and planting it outdoors. He has had almost a bushel of sweet potatoes from one vine, and he claims they are the easiest of all vegetables to grow. He leaves them in the soil as late as possible in fall, and then digs them up before frost, on a bright, dry day when soil is dry. He lets the roots dry in the sun for 2 or 3 hours, and then cures them for storage.

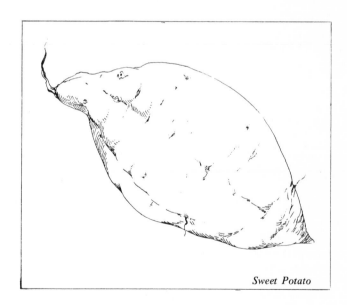

Sweet Potato

Problems: Rot, due to overwatering or poor drainage. Stunt or yellow dwarf disease. Due to poor seed stock. Grow yellow-dwarf free stock.

PUMPKINS

Where small space is a big problem, pumpkins are hardly worth considering. However, there is a bush pumpkin called Cinderella which grows 10" pumpkins

Pumpkin

Thin plants to about 1 inch apart. Water regularly so they won't be so sharp tasting as outdoor radishes. If soil gets dry the radishes get "hot," so put the fire out with daily watering. Make additional plantings every few weeks for a continuous supply of crispy radishes. Incidentally, the radish seed is a quick germinator, with lots of "pushing up" power. If you have trouble germinating such seeds as carrots, parsley, or parsnips, mix a few radish seeds with these slow-growers and see how the radish seed breaks up the surface crust. You can pull them out later.

Problems: Common complaint is bottomless tops. Due mainly to failure to thin out the seedlings while young. Be sure to thin 1 or 2 inches apart. Also be sure to pull up radishes while they are young and tender, to keep them from growing large and competing with themselves. Hot taste is another complaint. Most radishes have some nippiness in them. Excessive bite is usually due to hot, dry soil, so keep radishes watered constantly.

Radish

on bush vines like summer squash. You can grow it with only 6 square feet per plant.

Green Thumb Tips: Sow seeds 2 or 3 per "hill". Pull out one and let two grow. They need full sun and lots of water. A box 2' x 2' x 2' would make a satisfactory container if there is no other spot available.

Problems: Squash vine borers. Grub leaves "sawdust" material on ground. Carefully slit stem where the hole is and stab borer. Cover stem with soil and it will form roots. Prevent borers by spraying or dusting top and bottom sides of leaves with malathion or methoxychlor.

RADISH
(Raphanus saturis)

Once you raise your first crop of radishes in tubs or pots you will agree they are hard to beat! Radish is the fastest of all vegetables to grow from seed, many maturing in about 3 weeks. You have a choice between red, white, round or tapered.

Green Thumb Tips: Select an early type such as Cherry Belle, crisp and delicious, smooth and almost guaranteed not to "talk back" once you bite into it. It has short tops and a bottom as round as a marble. Icicle is a popular white radish with roots 4 inches long and nearly straight. It's our earliest long white radish. Champion, another good radish for containers, is round and brightly colored. Tops grow rather tall.

Radishes like a loose, humusy soil. Make successive sowings every few weeks for a continuous supply. They like lots of water, especially in hot weather. You may find that radishes do not form bottoms in late fall or winter. Research is showing that bottom formation can be associated to day length. Short days in fall may be responsible for some radishes forming bottomless tops. It doesn't always work this way, as we have had radishes in fall and winter — raised in our home and greenhouse.

Sow 2 or 3 seeds per inch and cover 1/2 inch deep.

RADISH—HORSE (HORSE RADISH)
(Armoracia rusticana)

Horseradish makes a good item for hotbed or coldframe, or a spot near the drain spout. You can buy roots from any seed house. A good variety is Maliner Kren.

Green Thumb Tips: Plant in any spot that is moist or in a pot, or in the coldframe. Roots are hardy and can be left in the ground all winter. Horseradish loves organic matter plus water. Heavy soil makes crooked roots. After the tops make good growth, dig up the roots, cut tops off, and replant the tops in soil. They will root and form new plants. We have never seen horse radish form seeds.

Problems: None.

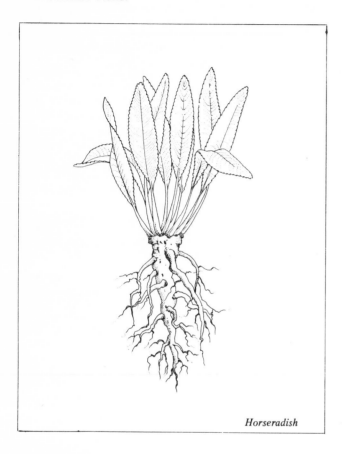

Horseradish

RHUBARB

(Rheum rhaponticum)

Here's one crop that really responds to culture in a coldframe. For years we have enjoyed sweet juicy rhubarb "pieplant" stalks in late winter and early spring by growing it in a coldframe which traps the sun's rays and brings the new growth on ahead of the normal season. However any spot available can be made into a rhubarb bed.

Green Thumb Tips: A simple way to force rhubarb is to use your portable hotbed or coldframe. Place the structure over the clump and cover with a blanket. Light is not essential or desirable. When grown in darkness or semi-darkness, the stalks get a nice color and quality, and the leaf blade expands to some extent. Note: Never eat the leaf as it contains calcium oxalate crystals and can be toxic. Some gardeners dig up rhubarb roots and bring them in the cellar or any dark or semi-dark location and force the stalks this way. Work in ample amounts of rotted cow or horse manure or peat moss into the soil. If none is available use ample amounts of

rotted compost of leaves and/or garbage. Rhubarb is a humus lover.

The roots are placed on the floor or in a box as close together as is feasible. Soil is scattered and worked over the roots to a depth of 3 inches or so, in between the clumps and around the rhizomes. Keep the soil moist, but not soggy. Best temperature is around 60 degrees. Higher temperatures bring the crop on earlier, but we think the color and quality are not as desirable as when you force rhubarb at lower temperatures. At temperatures of 45 to 50 degrees growth becomes too slow.

Rhubarb roots need to be left outside or frozen in fall before they can be forced. Freezing is essential for forcing, and light freezing is better than heavy or severe freezing. If you happen to live in the south, you can buy rhubarb roots and keep them in a cold storage freezer below 32° but no less than 10 degrees for two weeks before forcing. Severe freezing (2 weeks below 10 degrees F.) can reduce the yield. After roots have been forced in this manner they should be planted in the ground so that they can make good leaf growth to support a yield for the next season.

You may prefer to leave your clumps of rhubarb in a permanent location and have it produce at the normal time, without the aid of a hotbed or coldframe. If you have a spot which is 2 feet by 2 feet and gets sun part of the day, you can grow a clump of rhubarb and enjoy this vitamin filled herb.

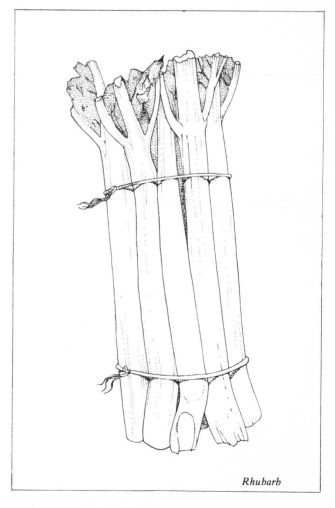

Rhubarb

Problems: Green stalks, due to variety. Choose the pink type such as Valentine, real red and sweet. Canada Red is said to be the reddest of all rhubarbs, juicy stalks are red all the way through and tender. Do not require peeling. A green stalked variety will usually stay green, although sometimes temperature will affect color of stalks. The new varieties stay red and are much sweeter than the older types.

Rutabaga

RHUTABAGA

(Swede Turnips) *(Brassica napobrassica)*

Here's a good one for the coldframe, but it can be grown in containers or any spot that gets full sun; although, the vegetable is unknown to most gardeners. It is similar to the turnip and culture is same as for turnip.

SALSIFY

(Tragapogon porrifolius)

Also called "Vegetable Oyster," salsify is a vegetable you should get to know. It's another good one for the coldframe or any sunny place where it can be left into the winter, and can be eaten in late fall, winter or early spring.

Green Thumb Tips: Sow 2 or 3 seeds per inch in rows 2 inches apart, cover 1/2 inch deep. Thin seedlings to about 2 inches apart. Salsify is hardy and can be dug up any time. Cover them with straw and dig them as needed. Some gardeners dig them in fall, trim off the tops at least 1 inch above the root, and then store them in moist sand in the cellar. They can also be stored in the coldframe, if covered with leaves or straw, just as you would store beets.

Problems: None.

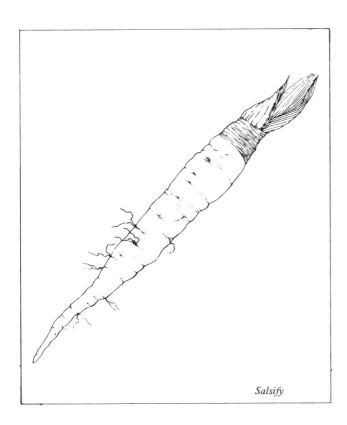

Salsify

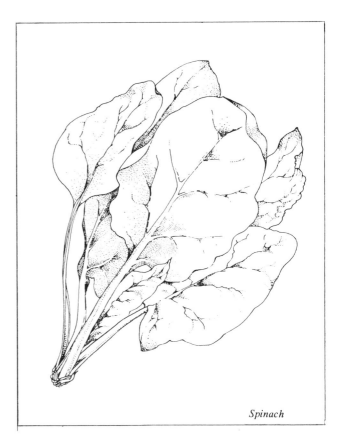

Spinach

SPINACH

(Spinacea oralacea)

This is one of the so called "potherb" crops, grown for foliage. Spinach does best in cool temperature, meaning it is suitable for the spring and fall in the coldframe or in boxes in protected spots. It is seldom grown in summer since it does not do well in hot weather. In the coldframe it will grow fine if you start early. Start plants indoors in pots and transfer them to the coldframe. Best varieties are Viking, an early, large long-standing variety that grows fast. Winter Bloomsdale takes heat better than most spinach types and is slow to "bolt" or go to seed, since it is tolerant of heat and cold. It is also resistant to blight. Its thick leaves are crumpled or "savoyed" and very attractive.

Green Thumb Tips: Start seeds in peat pots of "Jiffy" Pellets and transfer to coldframe. Or sow seed directly in soil of coldframe. You can also sow in pots or boxes at the rate of 2 or 3 seeds per inch, cover 1/2 inch deep and thin to 3 inches apart. Successive plantings will give you a supply throughout the season.

Problems: Blight. Select a blight resistant type such as Winter Bloomsdale.

SPINACH, NEW ZEALAND
(Tetragonia expansa)

This is not a true spinach, but is an excellent substitute for it, making an ideal summer greens. This "spinach" is killed by hard frost outdoors, but thrives well during the hottest weather. Grow it in the coldframes or in pots, boxes or other containers. We grow it in tubs or pails since the plants take up considerable space. We grow 1 plant per 12 inch pail or 3 plants per 24 inch tub. Spread plants at least a foot apart, in the coldframe or in spaces in the flower bed. Pick off the tender new leaves at the tips of the branches, and the plants will continue to produce succulent new growth all. summer, fall and winter.

New Zealand Spinach

Green Thumb Tips: Seed germinates slowly and we like to soak it for 24 hours before sowing. Sow 2 or 3 seeds per inch, cover 1/2 inch deep and later thin seedlings and transplant so that they each have about a square foot to grow in.

Plants like a uniform supply of water for tender leaves which branch freely.

Problems: Moldy leaves. Keep foliage off ground, and avoid splashing water on it.

SQUASH
(Cucurbita)

Like summer squash for winter eating? Try the Aristocrat, a 1973 All America Winner, or Early Prolific Straightneck. Bush vines take up less space and produce smooth medium sized fruit of good appearance. Zucchini Elite is a fine hybrid, but its vines are apt to take up a lot of space, unless you train them to a wire corset. If you don't have room for both cucumbers and zucchini, then grow the zucchini since you can slice it and use it exactly like cucumbers, and it can also be cooked, using a number of delicious recipes.

Harvesting: We harvest zucchini and other summer squash when small, about 6 or 8 inches. At this stage they can be stuffed, pickled, or eaten raw. If you keep fruits picked it will make the vines bear a longer period of time.

For mini-gardeners who want to grow winter squash, a good winter acorn squash is Bush Ebony, developed by Dr. Henry Munger of Cornell. Its semi-bush vines spread about 4 feet and can be trained on a trellis. Although the vines are smaller, they produce as many fruit per plant as standard acorn squash. Gold Nugget has bush vines, and this along with Bush Ebony are best for pocket gardens culture since they do not have the large running vines most winter squash have.

Gold Nugget has fruit size of a softball, orange skin, and is just right for serving in the shell. We bake them whole and remove seeds at eating time. We then spread seeds on a pan, salt and butter and bake 20 to 30 minutes longer at 250 degrees. They taste like popcorn.

Green Thumb Tips: For summer squash (either green or yellow types) or patty pan you can start seeds in tubs or deep boxes and leave one plant per square foot or three plants per tub (about 2' by 2'). We start our seeds in peat pots at the same time as we do our melons and cucumbers. This way they bear sooner and we have squash for a longer period. Summer squash are underrated. They are prolific, nutritious and delicious. We recommend you grow bush types of both zucchini and patty pan (we love these fried).

For winter squash, sow 3 or 4 seeds per large tub, or 4 seeds per square foot. Cover 1/2 inch deep, and thin seedlings one per square foot.

Keep plants well watered but be sure soil is well drained. Note: When harvesting winter squash such as Gold Nugget or Bush Ebony, make sure they ripen thoroughly — until the shell is quite hard and mature.

Problems: Squash and pumpkins have a few troubles such as mosaic and squash vine borers. Blossom-drop is nothing to worry about. Squash and pumpkins produce 5 to 10 male blossoms to 1 female, and only a small per cent of the female blossoms naturally develop into normal fruits. The males and excess or unfertilized female flowers dry up and fall, their love life shattered forever.

White flies: Resort to biological control Encarsia parasite which attacks the nymphs and pupae of the white fly.

Squash vine borer is the most common pest of pumpkins, summer and winter squash. Control by dusting the vines with malathion or methoxychlor, making sure you cover under sides of leaves. In the fall pull up vines and burn if borers have been a serious problem. If borers have entered the vine, slit stem carefully with a sharp knife to remove the larva.

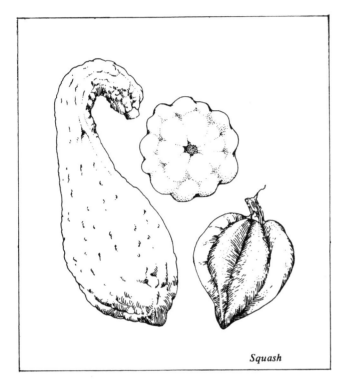

Squash

TOMATO
(Lycopersicon esculentum)

Of all the vegetables grown in the home or outdoors, none of them are as popular as the tomato. With our modern varieties you can grow tomatoes in any sort of container outdoors or in, on the window sill, bay window, or on the sun porch. Try both the small fruited and the standard tomatoes. The smaller varieties include Pixie, a fast growing, early ripening tomato, growing 18 to 24 inches high or so. It bears heavy crops of bright, smooth attractive fruits, the size of a golf ball. Fruits ripen 52 days from the time plants are set in the pot or bench. Other smaller varieties include Tom Thumb, Tiny Tim, Patio, Small Fry and Presto. Presto produces large amounts of fruit 1-1/2 inches across, over a long period and has comparatively small vines. It has an excellent flavor as does one called "Gardener's Delight" from the George Ball Company.

Other small fruited tomatoes include Red Cherry, Red Pear (pear shaped, 1 inch in diameter), Yellow Pear,

tiny yellow (fruit not acid) and Yellow Plum, ideal for preserves. A mild tomato, Roma VF is both verticillium and fusarium resistant, produces pear shaped, 2-1/2 to 3 inches long and about 1-1/2 inch in diameter. This is not an acid tomato and is useful for blending with regular types.

A good tomato of the standard size varieties for those who cannot eat "acid" types if the Sunray, a yellow-orange fruited type, meaty and tasty. It produces large crops of fine smooth fruit, the rich golden-orange flesh being ideal to "perk up" salads.

There are novelties such as Snow White (white when it's ripe), Evergreen (green when fully ripe) and the blue tomato, but we feel you should devote valuable space to bread and butter types.

There is no one best variety of tomato; some prefer the hybrids for heavy yield in limited space. Look over your favorite seed catalogs and see their selections. You can prevent a lot of disease by looking for the letters V, F, or N after each variety. They stand for Verticillium, Fusarium or Nematode resistant. Heinz 1350 for example, is disease and crack resistant, while Glamour is crack-resistant. It's practically impossible for Glamour to develop skin cracks which means you don't have to do much cutting away of skin blemishes.

Green Thumb Tips: To get a crop, you have two choices: Start your own plants, or buy them started from a greenhouse. Why buy plants when you can grow your own — and be sure of getting the variety you want? Sometimes fruit stands conveniently change stakes with names to please a customer who wants a certain variety. Half the fun is in growing your own from seed.

First, keep in mind that there are early, mid-season and late tomatoes. It might be a good idea to have all three types so you will have tomatoes coming along at different times. Mix up a flat of your favorite soil mix,

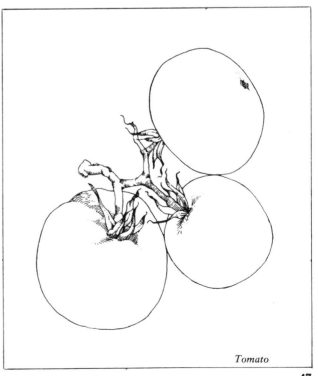

Tomato

or use any of the commercial ones on the market, such as "Jiffy-Mix", Pro-Mix", etc. These are uniformly mixed, have lots of organic matter in them, allowing for easy removal of seedlings. You don't break off roots when you transplant.

Sow seed thickly and cover 1/4 inch deep, using peat or same material used for starting. Or you can start plants in "Jiffy-7" Pellets or peat pots. You plant pots and all in the containers, without any transplanting. They can be grown in hanging baskets, too. In pellets or peat pots, sow 2 seeds in each.

Seeds should be watered thoroughly, and a plastic sheet placed over them to prevent drying out. Remove plastic as soon as seeds sprout. Successful germination takes uniform moisture. Once sprouted, seedlings will die, if they dry out. Most germinating seed needs heat, around 75 to 80 degrees F. Low temperatures, especially at night cause seed to rot, hence poor germination.

After seeds are up remove any covering, and put them in a bright spot for full sun. After they have developed their first set of true leaves and are about 2 inches high, transplant them into individual pots to be placed in containers as soon as weather permits. The advantage of starting them in "Jiffy-7" pellets or peat pots is that you do not have to transplant them. You plant pot and all. You can grow patio type tomatoes in window boxes or in pots or pails. Most cherry types will produce if grown in as little as 50 cu. inches of soil per plant. We grow standard size varieties in half barrels with wire corset supports. We have excellent results with four plants in a 2 foot diameter barrel which is 2 feet deep. Be sure to drill holes for drainage.

A note about transplanting seedlings from seed flat to individual pots or containers. Make sure the soil is moist. Take a trowel and loosen up a block of seedlings. Then "tease" a seedling out, without breaking roots, and set it in a pot of soil (1/3 each of sand, peat and loam, carefully mixed and moistened). Take a pencil or wooden stick, make a hole in the soil and insert the seedling. Do your transplanting on a cool day, or out of full sun. Water them well. Be sure never to transplant seedlings into a dry soil.

Don't forget potted or tubbed tomatoes need support. Commercial growers train their plants up a strong string. We use a wire fencing (concrete reinforcing material with 4 in. mesh, and obtainable at any lumber yard). Strips of cloth or binder twine are good for tying vines to the wire.

Prune Tomatoes? Some growers like to prune or sucker their tomatoes, others don't bother. Both schools bring good crops. In the single stem system of pruning all the suckers of side-shoots are removed and the plant is trained to a single stem.

As the plant grows note there are shoots which appear in the axils of leaves (that's the angle where the leaf attaches to the stem). These shoots are called "suckers" and some gardeners like to remove them when 2 to 4 inches long. Take your thumb and forefinger and grasp them, pulling outward and downward. Remove them while still small. Most gardeners prefer to pull the suckers rather than cut with a knife since there is less chance of transmitting virus diseases. Stop pruning or suckering your plants after the first crop of tomatoes is produced — we don't bother to prune our tomatoes and feel we get good yields.

Feed your tomatoes once every 3 weeks and keep the soil moist but not soggy at all times. Night temperatures either below 60 degrees or above 80 degrees and day temperatures above 90 degrees are unfavorable to fruit set.

Cross-Pollination: If you grow indoors tomatoes need your help in cross pollination, if you want a heavy crop of fruit. Indoors they are sheltered from wind and insects and thus often do not get pollinated. Outdoors, the vines are constantly being stirred by breezes or moved by bees and pollen grains get distributed to the right places. You can shake each plant and touch each blossom to effect pollination. If you have a cat use his tail (don't chop it off!) to transfer pollen from one blossom to another. If you can't use a cat's tail, use a camel's hair brush to transfer pollen.

Problems: Poor fruit Set: too high or too low day or night temperature. Night temperatures between 70 and 75 degrees and day temperatures between 80 degrees and 90 degrees are best for fruit setting of most varieties of tomatoes. These temperatures are not only best for setting, but produce larger fruits. Tomatoes growing in tubs or on the patio, can be protected at night with blankets or plastic sheets. Lots of Vines; Little Fruit: Large vine growth often results in poor fruit setting. Maintain a good level of moisture in the soil for good fruit set and better yields. Blame temperature extremes for erratic yields. Also, poor light due to cloudy weather reduces photosynthesis, resulting in low food production. On cloudy short days of fall and winter it is often difficult to set tomatoes indoors, regardless of the temperature. It is interesting to note that varieties vary in their ability to set fruit. For example, Fire Ball and Pearson will set fruit even under somewhat adverse conditions.

Too much nitrogen will cause lots of vines and fewer fruits. Generally speaking, if you add extra nitrogen, it should be applied after the main portion of the fruit on the plant has set. Earlier applications will often result in all "bush and no fruit."

Blossom End Rot: If tomatoes have black leathery spots on the bottom of each fruit, it's blossom end rot. It's usually due to shortage of moisture, that's why most gardeners mulch their tomatoes with straw, etc. to maintain moisture. Some varieties such as Rutgers and Marglobe are resistant to blossom-end rot.

Cracking of Tomatoes: Some varieties crack easier than others. You have three types of cracks: radial, concentric and entire skin cracking. You get it more often after plants are allowed to get dry, than when you water copiously. Glamour and Heinz 1350 are good varieties and are resistant to cracking.

Yellowing of Foliage: May be due to excess lime, or lack of iron or shortage of nitrogen. Test soil for acidity. Feed to overcome nitrogen deficiency.

Leaf Mold: Yellowish or green spots on foliage. Worse in cloudy weather. Avoid watering leaves, especially at night and ventilate during dark, cloudy days.

Leaf Roll and Curl: Worse on plants in poorly drained soil. It also shows up on plants which are allowed to go dry, then suddenly watered.

Leaf Wilting: Due to a fungus that lives in the soil. Old soils, used year after year, may harbor the fusarium fungus. Grow resistant varieties such as Manalucie, Homestead, Heinz 1350, Campbell 1327 or New Yorker and try to change the soil.

Mosaics: (yellows, streaks), leaves mottled, crinkled, puckered, deformed. Due to virus, often spread by people who smoke or handle tobacco. Never handle tobacco while working with tomatoes, potatoes, eggplants, petunias, or other members of the same family. Smokers about to handle tomato plants, dip your hands in whole milk or skim milk, or 4 ounces of dried skim milk per quart of water, every few minutes. Why? The milk de-activates the virus.

Insects: Aphids, cause leaf tips to curl. Spray with nicotine sulfate. Slugs: Set beer traps, or alcohol in flat dishes. Inspect plants at night and catch snails. Stoker ashes, or wood ashes, or sand around the base of plants discourages slugs. White Flies: "Flying Dandruff" found on undersides of leaves. Introduce some parasites (Encarsia). (See: Biological Control) Clean up weeds under the benches, because certain pests such as whitefly thrive on weeds.

For general tips on preventing diseases on tomatoes and other vegetables: see section on Pest Control.

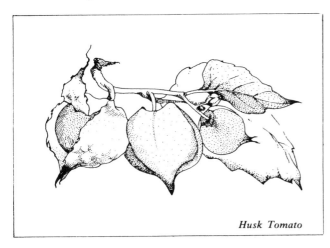

Husk Tomato

TOMATO, HUSK
(Physalis pruinosa)

While not a true tomato, the husk tomato is a low, bushy plant that bears a papery husk-like structure enclosing a yellow or greenish 2-celled berry which tastes something like a tomato (if you use some imagination). Also called strawberry tomato, Dwarf Cape gooseberry, or ground cherry. Don't confuse this with the cherry tomato (a true tomato) that grows the size of a quarter to a golf ball.

Green Thumb Tips: Start seeds in peat pots. Grow in pots, 2 per 10" pot. Fruits make a good ground cherry preserve and pie.

Problems: None.

TURNIP
(Brassica rapa)

This is a cool season crop which can be grown in the coldframe, containers, or spaces among other plants in late fall. During the fall months when fresh vegetables are scarce, you can depend on turnips to give you a lift. Turnips all have the same cultural tips as rutabagas. We

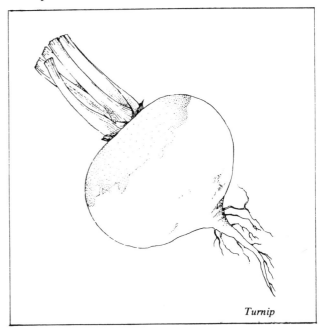

Turnip

recommend you grow a variety called Just Right, a clear white rooted turnip that matures in 35 days. This is the first true F1 hybrid, a product of the Japanese plant breeders. It is a fast grower. We have sown seed in late September and had a fine crop in November. The deeply cut leaves are fine for greens and the bottom is nice and round, shapely, very mild and tender. In fact, we prefer Just Right turnip to radish and eat them raw. There are other, larger varieties for turnip lovers so let the seed catalog be your guide.

Green Thumb Tips: Sow seed of Just Right in fall, 3 or 4 seeds per inch; thin seedlings to about 2 inches apart. Do not sow seed in early summer as it produces seed stalks if sown that early. It is a cool weather crop, and will stand moderate frost. Other turnips take longer and grow larger so allow more space. They can also be grown in early spring.

Problems: None. They come in the cool weather or fall or early spring when most insects aren't around.

WATERMELON
(Citrullus vulgaris)

"Ice box" watermelons were bred especially for people who have no room for giant melons. They can be grown on fences, in pots, or tubs if given a trellis for support. For a yellow-flesh variety try Golden Honey, or you can try a red-flesh type Hampshire Midget, or Sugar Baby, tiny icebox types. Another easy and small melon is the Takii Gem (prounounced "Tocky"). Bush type melons are available where a normal vine melon takes several feet to run; bush types can be grown in 1/4 the space.

Green Thumb Tips: Start plants indoors in peat pots or "Jiffy" Pellets three weeks ahead of the time that it is safe to set outdoors. We plant watermelon in half barrels

Watermelon

(2' x 2') about 4 plants per barrel.

Watermelons like it hot and they like plenty of moisture. Knowing when to pick a watermelon is a trick. Cool, wet conditions delay ripeness. Here are some indicators of ripeness: Brown tendrils on the stem near the fruit. A yellowish color where the melon touches the ground. A rough and slightly ridged feel as you rub your hand over the melon. Most varieties give a metallic ringing sound when they are green, and a muffled or deadsound as they get mature.

Problems: Blossom-end rot. Due to lack of moisture.

Increasing the amount of available gardening area is often possible through the use of window greenhouses. A variety of plants can be raised in these units, depending upon light needs, from the roof to floor level.

RAISING FRUITS IN CONFINED AREAS

If it seems strange to you that fruits can be raised in tubs indoors or outdoors, keep in mind that it's being done by hundreds of mini-gardeners. Here are a few fruits you can grow:

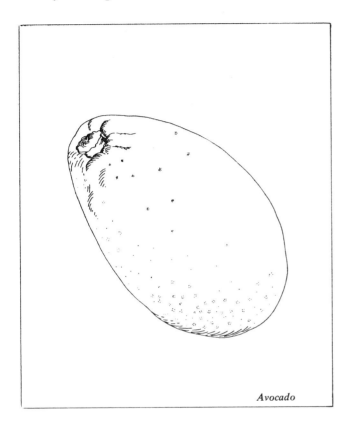

Avocado

Banana

AVOCADO

You won't be able to get fruit from an avocado, but you can enjoy the nice foliage from a plant started from a "pit" or seed. Some start the seed by placing the bottom half in a glass of water. We think a more fool-proof method is to pot the seed in a loose soil mixture. Set seed so upper half is exposed, water with warm water. After seed starts to sprout, keep it in a bright window.

BANANA

Believe it or not, one of our friends raised a 75 pound bunch of bananas in his home. Remember this: when ordering banana plants from your nursery, be sure to specify the edible types. There are many ornamental bananas you can grow, but few of them are edible. If you want edible types, stick to the Musa nana cavendishii.

Green Thumb Tips: Grow in tubs using a loose, humusy soil. Never let the soil go dry. A mixture of one part each of sand, peat and loam is good for bananas. Water the plant enough to keep the soil moist, never soggy. Grow in full sun. If grown indoors, do not let the temperature get below 60 degrees. Spray or syringe the leaves once or twice a week. Tubbed bananas can be grown inside in winter and moved outside during the summer months, as they are not hardy in climates where temperatures drop below 32°F.

Problems: Blackening of foliage. Due to overwatering or poor drainage. Browning of foliage is due to lack of water.

BLUEBERRY

Blueberries in tubs, pots or as ornamental landscape plants are well worth trying. The main requirement is a humusy, acid soil.

Green Thumb Tips: Order plants from your nursery. We suggest two or more varieties with different maturity dates so you can have fresh berries over a longer period. Jersey, Coville and Collins are good varieties to try. Use a soil mixture of one part peat moss and one part loam. Acid peat moss is what the blueberry needs for green leaves. Water the plants regularly and make sure drainage is good. Blueberries cannot survive under waterlogged conditions. During the winter months, you can leave the tubs outdoors, covered with straw or wrapped with burlap. Pruning blueberries consists of merely cutting off the short twiggy growth to allow vigorous new shoots to grow.

Problems: Birds eating fruit. Cover with cheesecloth when fruit starts to ripen. Yellowing of leaves is due to lack of soil acidity. Water plants with vinegar water, one tablespoon to a quart of water once or twice a week or you can use any of the acid products prepared especially for acid loving plants. These are available at garden centers.

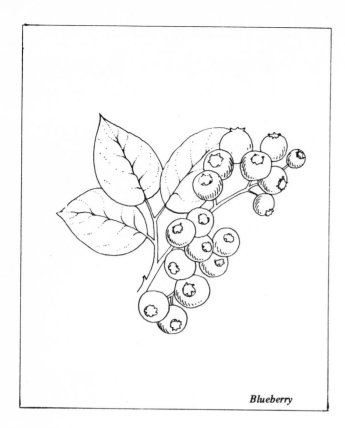

Blueberry

market baskets full of sweet mouth-watering dark, glossy cherries for eating from the bush, or for making pies, jam or jelly.

Green Thumb Tips: Buy a plant from a nursery and grow it in a tub or space against the wall or property line for landscape decoration. Plant is hardy but likes full sun. You may have to trim out some excess branches every other year. Just cut out any branches that criss cross or rub against one another. Be sure to leave no stubs. Prune branches flush with the main limb. Keep the bush watered, especially during the hot dry days of summer to prevent leaf scorch.

Troubles: None serious. Drying of leaves due to dry soils.

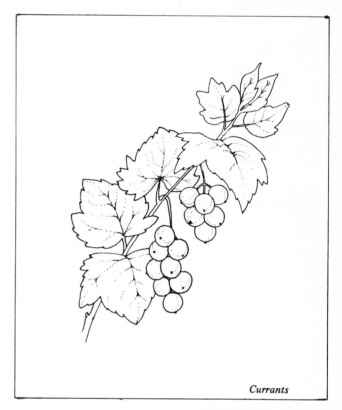

Currants

BUSH CHERRY (Hansen's)

If you're looking for an ornamental shrub that's attractive and still produces edible fruit, grow the Hansen Bush Cherry. It can be grown in tubs, or along the property line. The plant grows four to five feet tall and has white blooms in spring. In summer, it produces

CURRANTS

Everyone should have a currant bush in a tub, pot or spot in the garden. Currants do well on soils too wet for other fruits. In dry soils, currants suffer from premature falling of foliage and fruit. There's nothing any prettier than a currant bush full of bright red berries.

Growing Tips: Try a variety called Red Lake. Set plant in soil consisting of one part each of sand, peat and loam. Full sun is needed. Keep plants watered regularly for stimulating fat berries. Harvest when fruit is bright red.

Troubles: Curled leaves, due to aphids on underside. Spray with nicotine sulfate.

GOOSEBERRIES

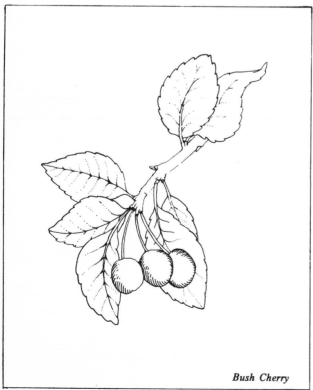

Bush Cherry

Gooseberries

Related to currants. Its culture is similar to currants. This is one fruit that remains to be "discovered". Once you've had jams or pies made from either currants or gooseberries, you'll wonder why you never raised them before. Gooseberries will grow in semi-shade or full sun.

Problems: Same as currants.

Date Palm

DATE PALM

The date palm (Phoenix longreiri) is a pygmy palm and it makes a good subject for the home because it likes a warm, sunny environment. Grow plants in tubs and have at least one of each sex because there must be a male and female tree for cross pollination to occur. Male and female blossoms are on different plants.

Green Thumb Tips: Most natural food stores have dates with seeds in. These seeds have not undergone heat treatment and are viable. Make a notch in the hard seed coat with a file or similar instrument and plant in a pot of sand and peat moss. Give a warm temperature — 80 degrees or so for germination, and keep the soil moist. When the plants are in blossom, transfer pollen from male to female blossom for fruit set.

Problems: Browning of leaves due to hot dry air, dry soils. Is not hardy outdoors below 33°.

FIGS, EVERBEARING

Everbearing Fig

Few things are more rewarding than an everbearing fig grown around your own premises. Fruit is sweet, delicious, good size, firm and meaty. Ideal for jams, canning or eating out of hand.

Green Thumb Tips: Best soil mix is one part each of sand, peat and loam. Grow in full sun. Bring the plant indoors in winter if temperature goes below 32°F. or give protection.

Did you know that you can start fig trees from seed found in store figs? Get some dried figs from your grocery store, remove seeds and plant them in a mixture of sand, peat and loam. Press seed lightly into the mixture, then dust a little peat over it. Water well, by placing the pot in a pan of water. Place a plastic wrapping over the pot's top to trap moisture and heat. Three months is required for seed to sprout. Young seedlings are very delicate, but will eventually grow rugged. Pot them in a three inch pot using a mixture of one part each of sand, peat and loam. Keep soil uniformly moist and grow in a bright window. When the tree is three or four feet high, plants will start to bear.

Many gardeners grow figs in tubs. These are brought indoors in winter, or are buried in a trench outdoors. Make sure you cover the trench with leaves or straw.

Troubles: None serious.

GRAPES

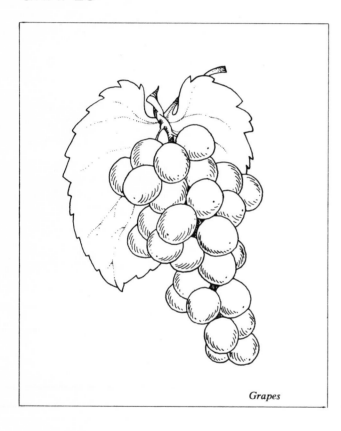

Grapes

Ever hear of growing grapes in a tub? It's being done. Some people grow them in hobby greenhouses, but they can be grown outdoors as well, and with great success. If you happen to have a fence along your property line, grow grapes for screen, ornamental and fruit effect. Try Concord, Interlaken Seedless or some other variety known to do well in your area.

Green Thumb Tips: Grapes like any type of soil. Set a vine in a tub or in the soil and train it to a trellis or fence. We have grape vines growing up our clump birch trees and we get excellent crops. With a new vine, prune the top back to two buds and as it grows, train it to grow up a trellis or on a fence. Grapes like full sun. They also like potash, so apply wood ashes — one handful around each plant, once a year.

After grapes are harvested, prune canes back so you

have two or three canes ready for next year's crop. Just pick out three fresh-looking canes (they're usually lighter in color) and cut out all the rest.

Problems: Downy and powdery mildew, whitish coating on foliage. Avoid splashing water on foliage.

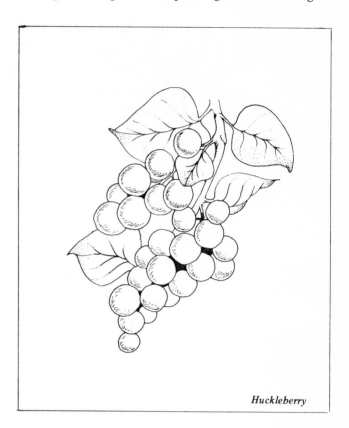

Huckleberry

HUCKLEBERRY, GARDEN
Solanum Nigrum

Also called Sunberry, this fruit rivals blueberries in use for pies and preserves. Fruit needs cooking to change the flavor and composition. Fresh berries are not tasty and for some people they act as a cathartic. Garden huckleberry yields an immense amount of fruit for the size of the plants.

Green Thumb Tips: Order seed from a nursery or seed house. Sow in pots and transfer your plants, two to each ten inch pot. Berries can also be grown directly in the ground if set two feet apart. Fruit to be cooked for pies or canning, can be picked a week after turning black.

Problems: None

JUNEBERRY (DWARF)

Several nurseries are offering a dwarf Juneberry for people who have limited space for fruit culture. Juneberry has large juicy berries which can be eaten with cream and sugar. Also good for pies, jam and jelly. Bush grows three feet tall and is ornamental, with white blossoms in early spring, followed by green berries that turn red, then deep blue when ripe. Burgess Seed and

Juneberry

MONSTERA DELICIOSA

This is often called a "swiss cheese" Philodendron but it is not a philodendron. The plant has deep green leaves up to two feet in diameter punched full of holes and scalloped on the outside. Fruit is yellowish green, cone-shaped from eight to ten inches in length. It is eaten like you would an ear of corn. Kernels when ripe are nearly transparent and filled with a sweet juice, having a delicate pineapple-banana aroma. Note: Don't eat it too near the cob as there are calcium oxalate particles present that will burn or irritate the gums or throat.

Green Thumb Tips: Buy plants from nurseries in California or start new ones from cuttings of old vines. Place a cutting in a pot of sand and peat and make sure you have a rib to each section. A rib is the spot where a leaf stem had been at one time and fell off as the vine became older. Grow in a semi-sunny window and keep the soil uniformly moist at all times. Do not overwater as it may cause the lower leaves to turn brown.

Problems: Browning of leaves due to overwatering or poor drainage.

Plant Company has a dwarf strain which grows three feet tall.

Green Thumb Tips: Mix a soil medium of one part each of sand, peat and loam. Plant in tubs or pots, along the property line. Tree bears fruit the second year.

Troubles: none serious.

PEACH, DWARF

Dwarf Peach

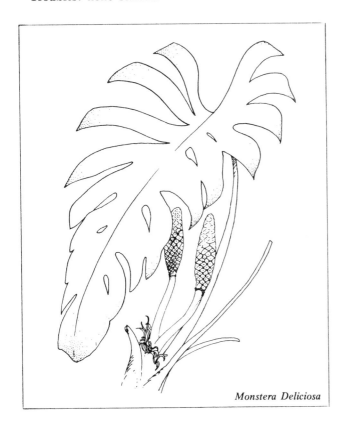

Monstera Deliciosa

Anyone pinched for space should give thought to growing a dwarf peach bush that grows four to five feet. It yields big, regular size deliciously flavored freestone peaches. The variety is called Bonanza.

Green Thumb Tips: Buy one of the trees from your nursery and grow it in tubs or large pots. Whether yours is a small yard or apartment, patio, terrace, suburban home, you'll have little trouble raising this peach. It likes a soil mixture of one part each of sand, peat and loam. Make sure pebbles are in the bottom of the tub for good drainage. Tree is hardy enough to grow in areas where regular peach trees grow. We suggest you bring yours indoors in winter, if you live in a cold region.

Troubles: Peach tree borer. Prevent by spraying tree with malathion in summer.

PINEAPPLE

You won't get rich or fat on the pineapples raised at home. Yet the fruit is just as sweet as that grown in Hawaii.

Pineapple

Green Thumb Tips: Buy a pineapple fruit from your supermarket — making sure you pick out the one that has a springy, green bunch of tufts. Cut the top off and place it in a shallow dish with a small amount of water. Keep it out of direct sunlight. Within four or five weeks the top will root. Once your top has rooted, pot it up in a loose mixture of sand, peat and loam. Let it grow in a sunny window and when a "red bud" forms — this is a cluster of tiny flowers (100 or so) which open into blue-velvet blooms. Each flower lasts for a day and each remaining flower develops into one segment of the fruit.

To get the pineapple plant to form into fruit here's a trick to try: (1) Place a plastic bag over the plant so air can be trapped inside. (2) Inside the bag place an apple (any variety will do). The apple releases ethylene gas fumes which are trapped by the plastic tent. These fumes are harmless to man, but will force the pineapple

to flower and form fruit. After the fifth day remove the plastic tent and soon you'll see new leaves starting from the center of the plant. And before long, you'll see rows of pineapple fruit appearing on the bottom of the new leaves. Put a stake in the pot to support the plant. When the pineapple is ripe, cut it off and serve it fresh.

Problems: Failure to set fruit: Give it the apple gas treatment. Failure of top to root can be due to plant being too old.

POMEGRANATE

Growing Tips: Pomegranates like a loose, humusy soil, our standard mix of one part each sand, peat and loam works fine. Keep it uniformly moist. These plants like full sun, and all the humidity they can get. Syringe the foliage once a week in a bath tub. The only pruning this item needs is during the summer when an occasional long shoot can be cut back. It needs to be outdoors in summer but be sure to bring it indoors before frost. Don't be frightened if it sheds its leaves in winter.

Problems: None serious. Red spider mites may come on leaves. Syringing with warm water will banish them.

Pomegranate

STRAWBERRIES

If you're hankering for a few fresh strawberries, grow them in hanging baskets or in a strawberry barrel. These are just the ticket for people with big gardening ideas, but little space. You can buy what is known as a pyramid circle which will hold fruits or vegetables. Made of heavy gauge, non-rusting corrugated aluminum, the pyramid will last for years. The bottom ring is six feet in diameter, and bands are five inches deep. They build up

Strawberries

to three terraces, with a built in sprinkler which connects to your garden hose. You can even get accessories such as support frames of aluminum rods, to support a netting made of durable marine-type material. The netting keeps out birds.

Green Thumb Tips: It doesn't seem to make much difference which varieties you grow. Some nurseries like to offer Ozark Beauty everbearing plants.

Strawberry barrels are fine for folks who lack space to raise a regular patch. Use any wooden barrel you may have, or buy one from a garden store. Choose a warm, sunny spot for a barrel or a pyramid. The barrel needs good drainage. For this, form a four inch diameter cylinder from screen or hardware cloth, obtainable from your local hardware. Place the cylinder in the middle of the barrel and surround it with six inches of coarse gravel, cinders, broken clay pots, etc., in the bottom, topped with finer soil mixture. Starting one foot from the bottom, bore a lot of holes in the barrel at irregular intervals, nine inches apart and large enough to hold a plant without cramping. A good soil mixture consists of two bushels of topsoil with one bushel of manure (rotted). For every bushel of the mixture, add three pounds of a balanced fertilizer such as 5-10-5. Planting and filling can be done at the same time. Start by covering the drainage sand with soil to level of first holes in bottom. Push the roots of the plants through each hole in the bottom row. Spread them out, and firm soil over them. Water sparingly. Repeat this planting and filling operation to the top of the barrel. In hot weather, you may have to water the barrel two or three times daily. Harvest fruit as it ripens. In winter, cover the barrel with burlap or sheets or cornstalks. If this seems unsightly, move the barrel into the garage, barn or cool cellar.

Troubles: Leaf spot. Nothing serious. Cat facing or nubbins on each fruit due to tarnished plant bug. Spray plants with malathion to check this pest.

HOME GROWN CITRUS

Are you surprised dwarf oranges, lemons or limes can be grown in and around your home? These amazing trees grow around two feet high, and produce usable, edible fruits. Foliage is glossy, and dark green. Fragrant white blossoms appear several times a year, followed by brilliant fruits that will remain on the trees for months.

Green Thumb Tips: If you're looking for edible citrus, do not start them from seed. Seed grown plants produce fine foliage and fragrant flowers but the fruit may be sour. Buy plants from a reputable nursery with the assurance you'll get edible fruit. Their plants are produced purposely for pot culture.

Start out with a loose, well-drained soil consisting of one part each of sand, peat and loam, fortified with one-half cup of bonemeal to each peck. Poor drainage will cause the leaves to drop, so do not overwater. Give the plants a good soaking and allow the surplus to drain away. Also, syringe the leaves on hot days to keep dust and insects away. About the only trimming or pruning that's needed is removal of any extra long shoots in spring or early summer. During the summer months most tubbed citrus benefit from a semi-shady spot outdoors. This summer treatment helps ripen the wood and assures fruit for late fall and winter. Be sure to bring the plants indoors before frost and place them in a sunny part of your home. A sunporch is ideal. All citrus plants like a cool night time temperature of 45 to 50 degrees. They also like full sun.

For fruit to set in your home, you'll have to hand pollinate the blossoms — a job normally done by insects

Calamondin Orange

and wind outdoors. Simply take your finger tip and go from one bloossom to another. This transfer of pollen will soon cause young fruit to form — probably within three days after pollination.

Here are a few of the edible citrus plants you can grow in your home and on your patio:

CALAMONDIN ORANGE

This miniature orange is definitely one for the home. You'll like the fragrant white flowers in addition to the edible one and one-half inch diameter fruits. It bears constantly and abundantly. The plant is thornless and has flowers and fruits in nearly all months of the year. A two-foot high plant does well in a ten inch pot, and it's not unusual to have 30 to 40 fruits per plant.

MANDARIN ORANGE

Excellent for growing indoors. Another dwarf is the OTAHEITE ("Oh-tuh-hee-tee") or TAHITI ORANGE, with fruit one to two inches in diameter. This minature version of the edible sweet orange is not considered too edible although the flavor is more like that of the lime.

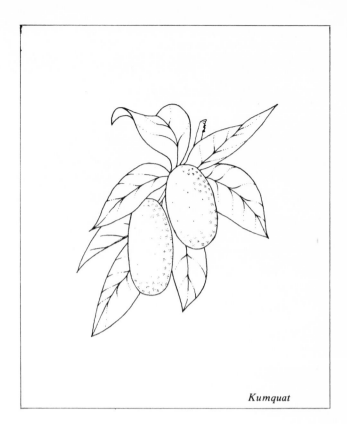

Kumquat

Mandarin Orange

KUMQUAT

Kumquat lovers should try one of the dwarf varieties suited for growing in the home. Fortunella margarita is a dwarf type that has fragrant flowers, followed by orange-yellow fruit about one inch in diameter. A variety that produces more flowers and fruit and is suited for

the home or home greenhouse is F. hindsii, a free-fruiting type which will reward your efforts with scads of fruit. It is highly ornamental but lacks juice. Fruits can be eaten, skin and all, fresh or pickled.

Green Thumb Tips: Buy started plants from a nursery and grow in pots or tubs. Grow them in full light outdoors in summer and bring indoors again in the fall.

Ponderosa Lemon

Problems: White fly and aphids. Wash with soap and water, or use nicotine sulfate. Be sure to cover undersides of leaves.

LEMON (Ponderosa)

Imagine making three to five pies from just one lemon grown in your home. It's possible — five lemon-meringue pies from one lemon. We've grown these lemons measuring five inches across, and weighing up to three pounds. What a sight it is to see these hanging on one plant. Ponderosa lemons take six months to reach edible size and when they start to bear, be prepared to prop the branches.

LEMON (Meyer)

Also called Chinese Lemon, it produces bright yellow, oval fruits equal to those in the supermarket. Plants have a few thorns, but not so many as the Ponderosa.

Persian Lime

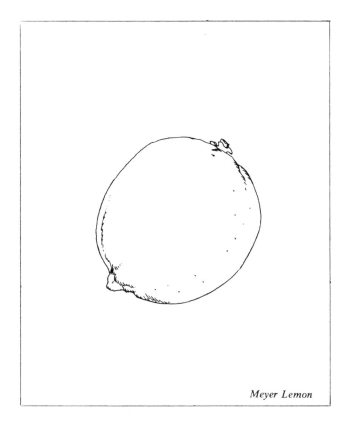

Meyer Lemon

LIME, PERSIAN

A fine dwarf citrus grown in tubs or pots. Plants grow to about two feet tall and the fruit is chartreuse-green and juicy.

DWARF FRUITS FIND VARIED USES

Dwarf Fruits, such as Armstrong Nursery's Bonanza Peach Bush, can be used in a variety of situations where space is limited.

A. Dwarfs can be used to line driveways or walks.

B. A decorative container plant placed on a patio can provide fruit and beauty.

C. Dwarf fruits can be used similarly to shrubs as accents against a fence.

D. Foundation plantings can be made with extremely dwarf, rounded varieties.

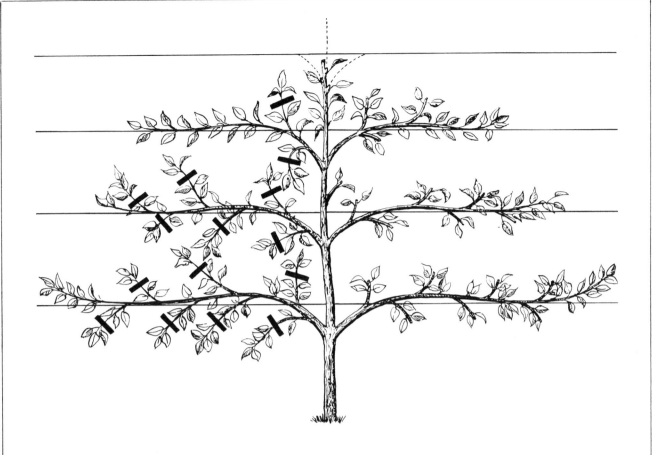

GROW FRUIT ON WALL OR TRELLIS

Who'd ever think you can grow fruit trees flat against the wall of your house or garage? Many are doing it, and the word for it is "espalier", pronounced "espal-yer" or "es-pal-yay", the training of certain trees to grow flat against trellises and other plane surfaces. For centuries the tree preferred for espaliering has been the pear but apples also are used.

Growing Tips: First, you must start out with dwarf varieties. Study the illustrations and you'll find it easy to do. Espaliered fruits will need trimming in the dormant season and during the growing season. Heaviest pruning is in early spring, just before sap flows, (called dormant or winter pruning). Summer pruning consists of shearing off or cutting back the side shoots at least once a month in July, August and September. In mild climates, extend this practice into November.

If you're not sure what shape to try, start in with the candelabrum type: To do this type of espaliering, the young tree's branches are restricted to a number (usually two, four or six) and trained to grow symmetrically, somewhat like a candelabrum. Branching is started low on the trunk. Unwanted shoots are pruned off and continually headed back. By tying the selected stems to the support as they grow, the branches are guided into the desired pattern. These trees can be espaliered against solid supports such as the sides of houses; they usually flourish best in full sun. Don't be discouraged with your first results. Try 1 or 2 trees first, and after you get the hang of it, you'll wonder why more people don't try espaliering, especially when they don't have the space to grow dwarf or standard fruit trees. Grow in full sun and during the dry spells make sure you water them as you would other plants.

Troubles: Wormy fruit. May be due to codling moth. Spray with Sevin when the fruit is about the size of marbles.

HERBS FOR THE MINI-GARDEN

Probably the nicest feature of herb gardening is that you can grow and harvest a tasty crop from your kitchen windowsill. Despite frequent shearing, chives will continue to produce luxuriant growth.

There's something romantic as well as aromatic in growing herbs. Seed houses report record sales of herbs last year. This year will produce an even larger number of "herb lovers." Herbs and spices led to the discovery of America. And now, Americans are discovering these plants.

People who grow herbs will tell you that a window garden full of herbs is a sight to behold. By growing several little pots of herbs right on your kitchen window or on the patio, you not only provide an interesting display, but supplement the family menu and budget as well. Most herbs which grow outdoors can be grown indoors with little effort. The only care they need is an occasional washing of the foliage to keep them fresh looking. Snip off any dead foliage and pinch the tops out so they'll be nice and busy. If insects happen to bother them, avoid spraying with anything but soap and water. If space permits, in summer you can put the potted herbs outdoors on the porch or patio and bring them indoors in fall. Or you can start herbs outdoors in window boxes, cement blocks or in among your flowers or vegetables. Then when fall comes pot them up so they can grace your home during dreary winter days.

Containers: The beauty of growing herbs is that you don't need a big garden or backyard to grow them. They do well in pots, hanging baskets and almost any other kind of container you can find outdoors. We've had best luck growing herbs in an ordinary cement block. Stand block so holes are vertical, fill the holes with loose soil (we like a mixture of one part each sand, peat and loam) and set plants in. By summer the blocks are practically covered with lush stems and foliage of the herbs. Your lumber yard handles the blocks. Plants are easily pushed out of the holes in fall and potted in six inch pots for indoor growing.

Light: Your kitchen or apartment window makes a fine "greenhouse" for raising herbs. If you don't have a bright kitchen window you can grow herbs with a little extra light. Go to your hardware store and get a 2-tube, 24 inch fluorescent light and fixture. Hook them up in the basement or in a window. If the room is dark, you'll need about 16 hours of light a day to keep your herbs growing lustily. There are light fixtures with adjustable legs which are ideal on a table or wide window sill.

How To Start: Retail stores sell seeds, plants as well as do-it-yourself kits for herb fanciers. The kits have a loose mixture, some with seed ready to sprout with water and heat. If a kit isn't used, you can sow seed directly in a pot of soil, using a 1 part each mix of sand, peat and loam. Cover the seed lightly and keep moist. When the seedlings are about 1 inch or so high, transplant them one to a four or five inch pot and place in a bright window. Keep the plants moist, but never soaking wet.

Harvest and Curing: Herbs can always be used in their fresh state but if you want to dry some for friends remember that herb flavor is due to an essential oil locked in small glands in the leaves, seeds, and fruits. Flavor is retained longer if the herbs are harvested at the right time and properly cured and stored. Young tender leaves can be used fresh any time during the season. For winter use, harvest when the plants begin to flower. Dry them rapidly in a well-ventilated darkened room. Tender-leaf herbs such as basil, costmary, tarragon, the mints, etc., which have a high moisture content should be dried rapidly **away** from light, if they are to retain their green color. If dried too slowly, they'll turn dark or mold. We dry ours on a cookie sheet placed in an electric oven, with door ajar, on lowest heat possible. In a gas stove, heat from the pilot light is usually enough. Without a pilot light, turn oven on at lowest heat possible and dry the herbs for two or three hours. The less succulent leaf herbs such as sage, rosemary, thyme, and summer savory — which contain less moisture, can be partially dried in the sun without affecting their color.

After herb leaves and seeds are dry, place in glass or metal containers which can be closed tightly to preserve odor and flavor. If yours are transparent you can paste labels around to make them opaque or store them in a closed cupboard to preserve color and flavor.

Watercress

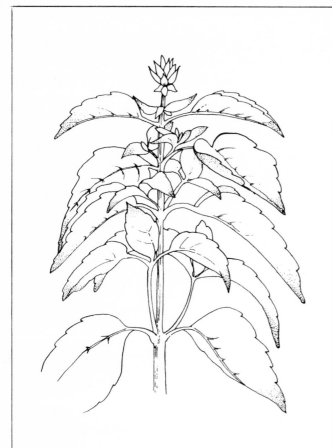

Basil

Chives

Dill

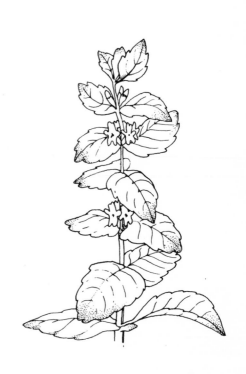

Lemon Balm

Lemon Verbena

Sweet Marjoram

Nasturtium

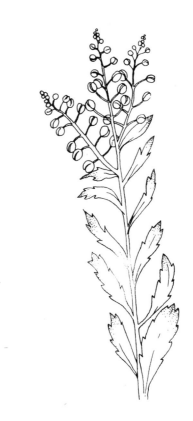

Peppergrass

Rosemary

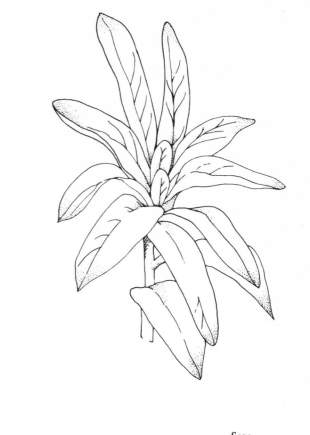

Sage

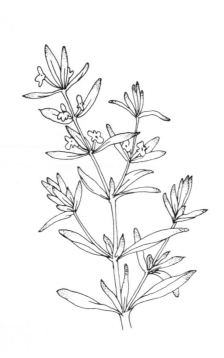

Savory

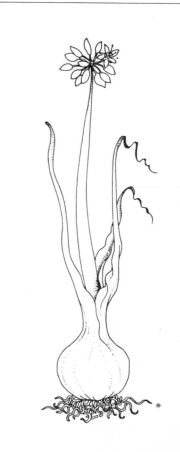

Shallot

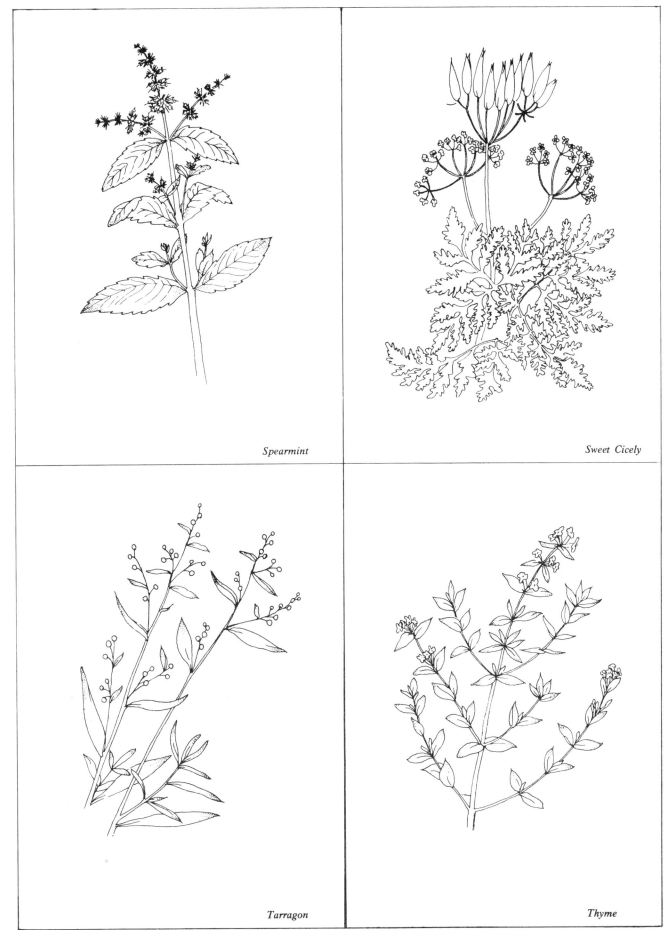

Spearmint

Sweet Cicely

Tarragon

Thyme

HERB	GROWING TIPS	OUTDOOR USES	INDOOR USES	HARVESTING AND CURING
BASIL	Sow seed in well drained soil. Likes full sun and ample water. 1 plant takes about 4 sq. inches of space.	Dark opal has purple-bronze leaves, spikes of lavender flowers Good in flower beds, attracts bees.	Good in flower vases. Use fresh or dried in cooking.	Cut 6" above ground when plants flower. Strip leaves and flower tips. Store in opaque jars.
CHIVES	Sow seed in spring, or buy started plants. Likes full sun, loamy soil. Snip off flower heads as soon as they form. A clump can be grown in a four inch pot.	Onion-like perennial handsome as border plant or in rock garden. Lavender blooms useful in vases.	Use in omelets, salads, cheese, soups and appetizers.	Cut leaves as needed. Bring pot indoors in fall and grow for winter use. Chives can be frozen.
DILL	Sow seed in spring or late fall in full sun. 1 plant can be grown in a 6 sq. inch space.	4 ft. annual which may need staking for wind protection.	Cheese, eggs, pickles; seeds in soups, gravies, vegetables.	Pick whole sprays and hang upside down to dry
FENNEL	Sow in May and thin to 6" apart. When plants are half grown, draw earth up to them to blanch the bulbous stalk.	Grown as an annual.	Valued for its anise-like flavor cooked or in salads.	Plants mature in 60 days and are dug. Seeds used in cookies, cheese and with vegetables.
LEMON BALM	Hardy perennial. Sow seed in summer in full sun. 1 or 2 plants can be grown in an 8 to 10 inch space.	Handsome border plant, 3 ft. tall. Do not let self-sow from seed.	Valuable in seasoning.	Cut tips 2 or 3 times a season. Store in dark place after drying.
LEMON VERBENA	Start from cuttings. Grow in full sun and give ample water. Can be grown in 4 to 6 sq. inches of space.	Fine perennial, also makes good house plant.	Sachets, perfume, flavors fruit salads, jellies and beverages.	Pick tender leaves and dry.
SWEET MARJORAM	Start early and transplant out in spring; likes well drained soil. 1 plant needs about 5 or 6 sq. inches.	Annual, 15" high with gray foliage.	Eggs, sauces, soups, stuffings.	Use fresh, or dry leaves and store in opaque jars.
NASTURTIUM	Seed in pots, or in garden. Grow as hanging basket item, or train up around window casing. 2 or 3 seeds per 6" pot.	Showy annual, loaded with blossoms. Hanging basket and porch pot plant.	Flowers, seeds make good sandwich with mayonnaise. Leaves used as greens, as with watercress.	Dry seeds and use as capers. Pick leaves and blooms as needed.
PARSLEY	Soak seed in warm water for a day, plant outdoors in rich, well drained soil. Full sun. 1 plant needs about 4 sq. inches of growing space..	Neat plant 12 ' tall, used in front border or edge. Grow variety called "Perfection" for is finely curled leaves.	Use as garnish in egg dishes, meat sauces, salads & dressing. High in Vitamins. Most useful of all Herbs.	Cut as needed, or dry in oven. Or freeze by rolling stems and leaves into "cigars" and wrap in aluminum foil. Or dry in oven and keep in tight jar. Dig up clump in fall and grow in bright window in winter.

HERB	GROWING TIPS	OUTDOOR USES	INDOOR USES	HARVESTING AND CURING
PEPPERGRASS	Sow seed 2" apart in early spring and again 2 or 3 weeks later.	Fast growing annual.	Leaves have pleasing, pungent taste.	Cut when ready.
PEPPERMINT	Plant roots or runners in spring. Shade and wet soils are good. Can be grown in moist spot or in a 5 inch pot.	Spreads fast, keep in bounds with metal strips or grow in tubs.	Fresh or dried leaves in Jellies, desserts, beverages.	Cut stems in bloom, dry and store in tight jars.
ROSEMARY	Start seeds indoors in spring, or root cuttings. Full sun, poor limey soil. Can be grown near steps or in a 5 inch pot.	Perennial 4 ft. high, blue fls. Needs winter protection.	Fresh or dried leaves in poultry, meats, or seafoods.	Cut leaves just before blooming period; crush and store in tight jars.
SAGE	Seed or cuttings in spring. Full sun, & well drained soil. Mulch in winter, remove dead wood in spring. 1 plant can be grown in a 5-6" space.	Shrubby perennial 2 ft. high; light-bluish fls. Fine addition to border.	Chopped, fresh leaves in cheese, pickles or sausage. Powdered leaves in stuffings.	Cut young tips dry in oven, pulverize lvs. and store in tight jar.
SAVORY	Sow seed in well drained soil, full sun. Grows fast. Winter savory has same care and uses. 1 plant needs 4 to 6 inches.	Annual, 18" high, bushy, with pinkish flowers.	Fresh leaves in green vegetables. Dried leaves in meats, turnips or cabbage.	Pull up plant and dry. Store leaves in sealed jars.
SHALLOT	Start from new shoots or cloves in spring. Rich, moist soil. Plant 2 inches apart and 2 inches deep.	Bulbous annual without much ornamental value.	Used in same manner as onion. Ideal for improving flavor of egg dishes.	Pull up when tops are yellow, dry 2 or 3 days. Cut off tops and store cloves in trays. Save some to plant next spring.
SPEARMINT	Same as for Peppermint.			
SWEET CICELY	Seeds planted in fall or spring, or divide parent plant. Partial shade, any type of soil. 1 plant needs about 8-10 sq. inches.	Fern-like leaves, fragrant white flowers; 2 ft. to 3 ft. tall.	Seeds have spicy taste, used with other herbs.	Pick seeds when green.
TARRAGON	Root cuttings in spring, or divide and set out divisions. Well-drained soil, full sun, or semi-shade. 1 plant needs about 6-8 sq. inches.	Handsome foliage, enhances the flower bed or borders.	Flavors sauces, salads, seafoods, stuffings.	Cut any time and hang in loose bundles.
THYME	Sow seeds indoors or outdoors. Thin to 1 or 2 plants to a 4" pot.	Fine foliage, dainty for rock garden.	Good flavoring for sauces, cheese dishes, pork, stuffing, soups.	Same as for savory.
WATERCRESS	Likes very moist soil.	Fast grower.	Leaves ideal in sandwiches.	Cut when ready.

HOW TO PRESERVE SURPLUS BOUNTY

HOME STORAGE

While freezing and canning are the common methods used in preserving food, winter storage of fresh fruits and vegetables still has its place. True, the old fashioned "root cellar" has gone with the modern home, being replaced mainly by freezers and canning. However, there are times when all of us want to store such items as potatoes, onion, squash, and other produce which taste better unprocessed. During this period of high food prices and shortage, it pays to save all surplus produce.

Temperature: Fruits and vegetables are living parts of plants. The cooler you can keep them, the better. Breakdown and decay is doubled with each 18 degree rise in temperature. Because increased temperature uses up food value of the produce, store it where the temperature can be kept within 10 degrees above freezing (32 degs.) if possible. A used "second" refrigerator in the garage makes an ideal storage.

Relative Humidity: This simply means the amount of moisture in the air. Fruits and vegetables are about 85% water. Unless the moisture content of the air is high, they'll soon shrivel, then lack quality, and may become unusable. Tossing water on a cellar floor from time to time is good in places lacking humidity. If you store produce in barrels or in a refrigerator you don't have to worry about maintaining the right amount of humidity.

For quick reference, we have grouped crops according to their best humidity and temperature:

Cool and very moist: Best temperature for beets, carrots, parsnips, salsify, turnips, rutabagas, kohlrabi, apples, is from 35 to 40 degrees. They like the highest humidity possible. These should be in piles or bins on a damp cellar bottom (a rare thing these days) or in containers with tight sides, such as barrels, tight boxes, galvanized garbage cans, crocks, etc. Cover them with bags of loose leaves or with newspapers.

Cool and moist: Cabbage, Chinese cabbage, celery, potatoes are best stored at temperatures from 35 to 40 degrees. Air should not be allowed to become moist enough to produce drops of water on the products. Crops keep best when placed on slatted shelves or in open slatted crates and bins.

Dry and cool: Onions, dry beans, squashes, pumpkins, and garlic like a temperature between 50° and 60° F. These like it drier. That's more important to them than is a cool temperature.

Pumpkins and squash keep better if you allow part of the stems to remain attached. Then place in a warm room at temperatures 80 to 85 degrees for about ten days. After that time, move them to a dry place where the temperature ranges from 50 to 60 degrees. Never store them where the temperature drops below 50 degrees. Acorn squash is an exception and can be stored at a temperature as low as 45 degrees. In this way, many squash can be kept until February. Do not pile squash in a tall box or basket. Spread them individually on a shelf.

Keeping Tomatoes Longer: Since the No. 1 crop you'll grow is the tomato, you'll be amazed to see how long you

A relatively moist, cool area can be prepared by burying a garbage can or barrel, placing vegetables inside and covering the top with bags of leaves or newspapers.

can store green tomatoes. It's possible to keep them up to six weeks. Remember, that the large, light green ones will ripen best in storage. Very small, immature tomatoes will not ripen well off the vine. Green tomatoes reach an eating-ripe stage in about two weeks if held at 65 to 70 degrees. If kept at 55 degrees however, it will take them about four weeks to ripen. Never store tomatoes for ripening where temperatures drop below 50 degrees. After tomatoes are fully ripe, they can be placed in the refrigerator. Peppers store best at temperatures between 45 and 50 degrees. Since they are more subject to drying, wrap them in plastic or use small plastic bags.

Storing Fruits: Winter apples such as Delicious, Spy, Baldwin, Jonathan, Cortland and many others are best adapted to storage. Apples picked too green store badly; if too ripe when picked, they rot readily. For best storage, most fruits should have a temperature as close to 32° f. as possible and a relative humidity of 80 to 85 percent. Apples and pears often pick up potato odors, but wrapping them in maple leaves in barrels will prevent absorption of such odors. Pears keep better if wrapped in newspapers and kept near 32 degrees. Grapes will keep longer if leaves are placed in among the clusters. Sheridan is a good keeping variety.

CANNING SURPLUS VEGETABLES

The home freezer has made "putting up" surplus produce a lot easier. However, canning is still popular and very useful. Many folks do not have freezers and even if they do there are some fruit and vegetables which taste better canned or pickled. There are two fool proof methods of canning: (1) The pressure cooker method, that requires a pressure cooker large enough in which to set pint or quart jars upright. (2) The hot water bath which requires a large pan and wire rack, with cover, large enough to surround and cover pint and quart cans with boiling water.

While fruit can be canned by hotwater bath, this method is no longer recommended for vegetables, except tomatoes and sauerkraut, because of botulinus toxin. Therefore, all other vegetables should be canned by the pressure cooker method.

Here are some hints on canning the most useful vegetables:

Note * asterisk before each vegetable means: add ½ teaspoon of salt for each pint, cover vegetable with fresh boiling water to one inch from top of the jar.

VEGETABLE	PREPARATION	LENGTH OF TIME TO COOK 1/2 Pts. & Pints 10 LBS. PRESSURE	Quarts
ASPARAGUS	Wash, break off tough portion, scald 3 min. Pack into clean, hot jars; process	25 min.	35 min.
*BEANS Wax, green	Wash, cut or leave whole. Scald 3 min. pack into clean, hot jars; process.	20 min.	25 min.
Lima	Shell and wash lima beans. Proceed as above.	35 min.	55 min.
*Beets (Young)	Wash, cook 15 min. or until skins slip off easily cut off root and stem. Dice or slice pack into clean, hot jars. Omit salt and add 1½ teaspoon vinegar to each pint to improve color and flavor. Process.	25 min.	35 min.
*Broccoli	Wash, soak in salt water, drain, scald 3 min. Pack into clean, hot jars and process. Has strong flavor and dark color after canning.	30 min.	35 min.
*Carrots (Young)	Scrub, leave whole or slice. Scald 3 min. Pack into clean, hot jars and process.	20 min.	25 min.
*Cauliflower	Same as broccoli. Has strong flavor and dark color after canning.	30 min.	35 min.
Corn	Use tender corn, handle quickly and in small amounts. Process as soon as picked. Corn loses flavor fast. Husk and remove silk. Cut from cob. Do not scrape cob if whole kernels are desired. Add ½ tsp. salt to each pint of corn. Cover with boiling water, bring to boiling point and pack into clean, hot PINT JARS, filling jars loosely to one inch of top. Stir to remove air bubbles. Process.	55 min.	85 min.
Egg plant	.Wash, slice or cube. Sprinkle lightly with salt, cover with cool water. Let stand 45 min. drain, pack into clean, hot jars. Cover with boiling water to within 1 inch from top. Process.	30 min.	40 min.
*Greens Beet Collard	Wash well, steam until stems are wilted; 2-4 minutes. Pack loosely into clean, hot PINT		

Containers For Processing: Jars used for mayonnaise, peanut butter, pickles, etc., marked "Duraglass," Ball (Anchor Hocking), or Kerr can be used for canning. Small mouth jars of this type may be used with a "63" lid. The "63" lid can be purchased wherever jars are sold. This is a vacuum-seal type lid.

Our thanks to the Home Service Department of Rochester Gas and Electric Corporation, U.S.D.A. and Cornell University for information used in our canning and freezing charts.

Dandelion **Spinach** **Swiss Chard**	jars, cut through greens with knife. Process.	70 min.	
PEAS	Use tender young peas and handle quickly. Shell, wash, and scald three minutes. Pack into clean, hot pint jars, add ½ teaspoon salt, cover with water to within one inch from top. Process.	40 min.	40 min.
Peppers, green	Wash, cut in half, remove seeds. Scald 3 min. Pack into clean, hot jars, add 1 Tablespoon vinegar and ½ teaspoon salt to each pint. Cover with water to within one inch from top. Process.	35 min.	
Pumpkin	Wash, peel and remove seeds. Cut in pieces. Bake steam or boil until tender. Add water to give **consistency** of pie filling. Bring to boil pack into clean hot jars. Process.	65 min.	80 min.
Sauerkraut	Make Sauerkraut. Bring to boil and pack into clean, hot jars add no water. Process		BOILING WATER BATH — — 30 min.
Squash (summer)	Prepare as for table use, cook 3 min. without adding water. Pack into jars in its own juice. Process.	25 min.	30 min.
Winter squash	Same as pumpkin		
Tomatoes	Wash, dip into boiling water and slip off skins. Leave whole or cut into quarters or halves and pack into clean, hot jars, pressing down so juice rises to cover tomatoes. Add 1 teaspoon of salt to each quart. We like to add a slice of onion and pepper on top of tomatoes in can. NOTE: Because of low acidity, yellow tomatoes should be processed under pressure.	Process 45 min. in boiling water bath. For pressure cooker use: 5 lb. for 10 min. 10 min.	5 lbs. for 10 min. 10 min.
Yellow Tomatoes	Under pressure only		
Tomato Paste **(for making sauces and soup)**	Combine 4 quarts tomatoes, 1 onion, 1 stalk celery, 1 bay leaf, 2 teaspoons salt, and ¼ teaspoon paprika. Cook until soft, strain, then cook until reduced to ½ volume or desired thickness. Pour into clean, hot jars and process.		30 min.

CANNING OF FRUIT

All fruits, including tomatoes, may be canned by the boiling hot water bath method. Canners are large covered pans having a rack or wire basket to keep cans from touching the bottom of the pan. They must be deep enough to hold cans so that the water bath covers the cans.

General recipe books, State colleges, the U.S.D.A., and public service agencies will have more complete instructions for canning fruit but we will give condensed instructions plus a time table to enable those who have excess fruit in their mini-gardens to be able to process them. Our thanks to Cornell University, U.S.D.A. and The Rochester Gas & Electric Corp. for information used in this chart.

Fruit may be canned with just plain water (for diabetics) or it is more tasty if canned in a syrup solution. This solution is made by adding sugar to water and bringing it to a boil. It is then poured over the fruit in the jar, within one inch of the top.

Acid fruits may require a heavy syrup, whereas fruit such as pears take a thin syrup. Peaches take thin or medium syrup, depending upon your sweet tooth.

Proportions for making syrup:

	Sugar	Water
Thin syrup	1	3
Medium	1	2
Heavy	1	1

It is a good idea to shake fruit down into the can so that it will be fully packed without forcing. A cup of syrup will usually be enough for a quart of fruit.

Below is a canning chart for fruits using the hot water bath. All fruit can be processed in a pressure cooker using 5 lbs. pressure for 10 minutes. For either method all fruit should be washed well and clean, sterile, warm jars should be used.

CHART FOR CANNING FRUIT BY HOT WATER BATH

Fruit	Preparation	Processing Time in Boiling Water Bath Pints and Quarts
Apples	We leave peels on our apples. Some like them peeled. Slice or quarter; boil one minute in thin syrup. Pack in clean hot jars, add boiling syrup. (To prevent discoloration, drop slices in solution of 1 t. salt & 1 T lemon juice to 1 qt. water before boiling)	15 min.
Berries	Wash, stem and pack berries in clean, hot jars. Add syrup (thin for most berries, thick for currants), process.	16 min.
Cherries Sweet Sour	Wash and remove pits, or if you prefer leave them in. Pack in jars and add boiling syrup. Thin for sweet cherries and medium or heavy for sour.	20 min.
Peaches	Some peel their peaches but we prefer to leave skins on. They add vitamins. We cut into quarters, remove stones. Prevent discoloration same as for apples. Use thin or medium syrup.	20 min.
Pears	Can be peeled if you prefer. We leave skins on. Cut in halves and core. Use same solution as for apples and peaches to prevent discoloration. Remove and pack into cans. Add boiling thin syrup.	20 min.
Plums and Prunes	Wash and pit if desired. Prick skins if left whole. Pack in jars, add hot medium syrup.	20 min.
Rhubarb	Wash, dice, pack in jars and add boiling hot thick syrup.	16 min.
Strawberries	Wash, hull, pack in jars. Shake down and either use a thin syrup or sift about ¼ cup of sugar per pint through the berries. In the latter case, no water is added.	20 min.

SAVE VITAMINS IN VEGETABLES

Don't be a hobbiest who grows vitamin packed vegetables in your greenhouse, house or yard but then dumps these vitamins down the kitchen drain. Here's what we mean: different parts of vegetables differ in nutrient content. For example, the leaf part of collard greens, turnip greens and kale contains many more vitamins than the stems or midribs.

If you remove the fibrous stems and midribs, you'll lose few nutrients. The outer green leaves of lettuce are more coarse than inner leaves, but have higher calcium, iron and Vitamin A value. Use the outer leaves whenever you can. When you trim cabbage, use the inner core too. The core is high in Vitamin C and so are cabbage leaves. Broccoli leaves have higher Vitamin A content than the stalks or flower buds. If broccoli leaves are tender, why not eat them? Keep them cool and moist until you can prepare them.

And when you boil potatoes, beans, etc. don't throw out the water! Use if for making soups, stews, gravies, etc., because the water is loaded with vitamins.

Harvesting: An important point is to pick vegetables at the proper stage. Harvest your vegetables at the proper stage of maturity to get the most out of your crop. (See section on Preserving Fruits and Vegetables)

The University of Minnesota suggests that you try to pick your vegetables just before you are ready to prepare them. Cook them as quickly as possible. Frequently preparing them in their skins. If you peel them, just scrape or pare thinly.

For example, summer squash are harvested in the early, immature stage when the skin is soft and before the seeds ripen. Don't pare summer squash. Just remove the stem and blossom ends.

Snap beans should be harvested before the pods are full size and while the seeds are about one-quarter developed or two or three weeks after the first bloom. Cooking time is shortened by cutting the beans lengthwise and cutting off the woody part.

Here are some signs indicating that your vegetables are at the proper stage of maturity and ready to harvest.

-**Beets ...** when 1-1/4 to two inches in diameter.

-**Broccoli ...** before dark green blossom clusters begin to open.

-**Carrots ...** when one to 1-1/2 inches in diameter.

-**Cabbage ...** when heads are solid and before they split. Splitting can be prevented by cutting or breaking off the roots on one side with a spade after a rain.

-**Cauliflower ...** before heads are ricey, discolored or blemished. Tie the outer leaves above the heads when the curds are two to three inches in diameter. The heads will be ready 4 to 12 days after tying the leaves.

-**Eggplant ...** when fruits are half grown, before the color dulls.

-**Muskmelon ...** when the stem slips easily from the fruit, leaving a clean scar.

-**Onions ...** from sets, when 1/4 to 1 inch in diameter for fresh table use. Select them for boiling when the bulbs are about 1-1/2 inches in diameter and for storage when the tops fall over, shrivel at the neck of the bulb and turn brown. Allow them to mature fully.

-**Peppers ...** when the fruits are solid and have almost reached full size. Allow red peppers to reach a uniform size.

-**Early potatoes ...** when the tubers are large enough to satisfy you. Small tubers are delicious mixed with fresh peas or beans. Skins can be scraped off. Mature tubers must be peeled and they keep better in storage.

-**Summer squash ...** when the skin is soft and before the seeds ripen.

-**Watermelon ...** when the underside of the fruit turns yellow or when snapping the melon with your finger produces a dull, muffled sound instead of a metallic ring.

The top-ten, most popular, garden vegetables (according to a survey of sales by leading American seedsmen) are: tomatoes, beans, sweet corn, cucumbers, peas, lettuce, radish, squash, melons, and beets. The list is greater for those who want to grow crops under glass. Don't be hampered by a lot of "Don't do this" rules. Try any vegetables you wish; so get busy and let yourself grow!

VEGETABLE FREEZING TIPS

vegetable	PREPARATION	SCALDING	PACKAGING
ASPARAGUS	Cut off tough part of stalk. Wash, place in colander. Immerse in boiling water.	Bring back to a full rolling boil. Drain.	Chill in ice water, drain, package, label, freeze.
BEANS, LIMA	Wash, shell, place in colander.	Bring back to a full rolling boil. Drain.	Chill in ice water, drain, package, label, freeze.
BEANS, SNAP	Do not use too mature or old beans. Sort, wash cut into ¾ inch pieces, or leave small beans whole. Place in strainer	Bring back to a full rolling boil. Drain.	Chill in ice water, drain, package, label, freeze.
BEETS, TINY, Whole	Place in colander or strainer.	Scald 3 minutes, drain, chill and slip off skins. Slice or dice.	Package, label and freeze.
	For greens, wash leaves cut off stems.	Bring back to a full rolling boil. Drain.	Chill greens in ice water, drain, package, freeze.
BRCCCOLI	Wash, trim off large leaves, woody stem. Soak in cold salt water, 1 teaspoon salt to 1 quart water. Split very large stems, place in strainer.	Bring back to a full rolling boil. Drain.	Chill in ice water, drain and wrap in bundles, package, label and freeze.
BRUSSEL SPROUTS	Remove outer bruised leaves, wash and soak ½ hour in 1 teaspoon salt to 1 quart water. Strain.	Bring back to a full rolling boil. Drain.	Chill in ice water, drain package, label, then freeze.
CARROTS	Wash, scrape or peel. Cut ¼ inch slices or dice. Strain.	Bring back to a full rolling boil. Drain.	Chill in ice water, drain, package, label and freeze.
CAULIFLOWER	Break head into flowerettes wash, soak in salt water 10 minutes, 1 teaspoon salt to 1 quart water. Drain, and put in strainer.	Bring back to a full rolling boil. Drain.	Same
CORN	Husk, remove all silk and wash. Put in strainer.	Bring back to a full rolling boil. Drain.	Chill in ice water and drain. Cut corn from cob, package and freeze. Seal in heavy duty aluminum or plastic bags.
(Corn-on-cob)	same as above	Same	
EGGPLANT	Peel and slice in ⅓ inch slices or dice in ⅓ inch cubes. Put in strainer.	Same	Chill by dipping first in solution of ½ cup lemon juice in 2½ pints cold water. Then chill in icewater, drain, pack and freeze.
CHARD, SWISS	Same as for beets		
HERBS Parsley, mint chives	Wash well and drain.	Scalding not needed.	Roll into a "cigar" and wrap with aluminum foil, freeze while wet.
Onions garlic, etc.	Do not wash. Freeze them on a cookie sheet.	No scalding.	Put in plastic bag.
PEAS	Shell, wash in cold water and drain in colander.	Bring back to a full rolling boil. Drain.	Chill, drain, package, freeze.
PEPPERS	Wash, halve, dice or slice, remove seeds. Spread on shallow baking pan. Slip into a large plastic bag and freeze 1 hour.	No scalding.	Put into small bags and return to freezer.
POTATOES Mashed	Mash by ricing to get as little air as possible.	No scalding needed.	Wrap in aluminum foil or freezer paper. Freeze.
PUMPKIN	Prepare same as winter squash.		Cnill (3 cups is enough for one 9 inch pie) label, freeze.
SQUASH summer	Select ones, before rind hardens, slice in ½ inch slices.	Bring to a full rolling boil. Drain.	Chill, drain, pack, freeze.
WINTER (Hubbard) butternut, acorn)	Cook until tender as for table use. Drain, force through sieve.	No further scalding.	Chill, pack in freezer boxes and freeze.

TOMATOES	Wash fruit and dry. (small cherry tomatoes freeze well in plastic bags)	No scalding.	Space out on a cookie sheet in freezer, do not let them touch each other. When frozen put in a plastic bag. They do not keep their firmness but are good for soups, stews, etc. Flavor and juice are there, and it's less work than canning.
(Tomato) juice	Wash, sort and cut in quarters or eighths, and simmer 5-10 min. Press thru sieve. Season with salt, 1 teaspoon to each quart of juice.		Pour into freezing containers with wide top, allowing 1 inch space at top of each quart. Seal and freeze.
STEWED Tomatoes	Peel and quarter ripe tomatoes cover, and cook until tender (10-20 min.) Place pan containing tomatoes in cold water to cool.		Pack into wide-topped freezing containers, leaving ¾ inch head space seal and freeze.

FREEZING FRUIT

Just about any fruit you raise can be frozen. Here are a few of the small fruits you can freeze:

FRUIT	PREPARATION	PACKAGING
Blueberries, Blackberries Raspberries Gooseberries	Sort, wash in ice water, handle carefully, drain thoroughly.	May be packed without sugar or syrup. Or use 1 pound (2 cups) sugar and 5-6 lbs. (10 to 12 cups) berries. Or, cover berries with medium syrup. Package and freeze.
Cantaloupe Watermelon	Peel, cut in thick slices dice or make melon balls.	Sprinkle with confectioners sugar. Pack in layers separated with waxed paper. Or cover fruit with medium syrup. Package, label, freeze. Serve slightly frosty.
Currants	Wash and stem.	Freeze whole currants without sugar or crush and add 1 pound (2 cups) sugar to 3 pounds (6 cups) currants. Package, label, freeze. Use for jelly making and preserves.
Rhubarb	Wash, trim, cut stalks, into pieces or make rhubarb sauce as for table use.	Pack with or without sugar or syrup. Use medium syrup or mix 1 pound (2 cups) sugar with 5-6 lbs. (10-12 cups) fruit. Package, label, freeze.
Strawberries	Sort, wash in ice water, hull, slice or leave whole.	Pack whole berries with medium syrup. Mix sliced berries with 1 pound (2 cups) sugar to 5-6 lbs. (10-12 cups) fruit. Stir only enough to dissolve sugar and allow to stand 20 min. Package, label, freeze.
	Whole strawberries for garnish; select perfect berries. Leave caps on, wash gently in ice water, drain well. Separate on shallow pan. Freeze.	When frozen, store whole berries in container. Remove berries as needed. Serve while still icy.

SYRUPS FOR FREEZING:
Sugar Syrup:
   Thin: 4 cups water — 2 to 3 cups sugar
   Medium: 4 cups water — 4 to 6 cups sugar
   Heavy: 4 cups water — 6 to 7 cups sugar

Sugar Pack:
   1. Use 2 cups sugar or less, if desired to every 5 to 6 pounds or 10 to 12 cups prepared fruit.

   2. Add sugar to fruit, mix lightly and let stand for 20 minutes to allow sugar to thoroughly dissolve.

Fruit is combined with sugar, or sweetened with syrup, for freezing. Fruit can be frozen without sweetening to be used for making jam or for diabetics. When freezing fruit for diabetics be sure to leave out the sugar.

INDEX